*Leap of Faith* by D  in exhilarating personal adventure and :y. The volume is not only the fascinating autobiography of an exceptional disciple of Christ, it also presents an engaging, personal insight into the international work of The Salvation Army over the past six decades. I highly recommend this book. It is informative, inspirational and challenging. One thing for sure, it will not be disappointing.
>*Commissioner William Francis*
>*Territorial Commander, Canada & Bermuda*

One of the phenomena of the post modern era is the rediscovery of the value of story.

How timely, then, that these personal reminiscences of a 20th Century Salvationist, originally written as a legacy for his own family should now be made available to a wider readership. The fact that Commissioner Dudley Coles chose an unusual approach adds interest to this well-written, informative and inspiring book. Enter the story with a desire to discover a Jesus encounter through his faithful witness.
>*Commissioner M. Christine MacMillan*
>*International Director for Social Justice (IHQ), New York, N.Y.*

Obviously *Leap of Faith* comes right from the author's heart. I found it exciting and touching, giving insights into world events otherwise known only through the media. This autobiography will have great value to Salvationists specifically, but should also appeal to a broader group of Christians – especially those interested in cross-cultural communications and missiology.
>*Ray Wiseman, co-author of When Cobras Laugh*
>*Fergus, ON, Canada*

DEDICATED TO

Our grandchildren:

*Samantha, Aidan,
Colin, Adam, Zachary,
Jordan, Ryan and Justin*

*Reach for the Stars
and always
Remember your Roots*

# LEAP OF FAITH

*A Reflection on Choices
that shaped an extraordinary life*

**Dudley Coles**

©2008 Dudley Coles

All Rights Reserved. No part of this publication may be reproduced, stored in a retrieval system, or transmitted in any form by any means, electronic, mechanical, photocopying, recording or otherwise without written permission from the author. Exception is granted for brief quotations embodied in critical articles or reviews.

Printed in Canada

PRO 08 09 08

Library and Archives Canada Cataloguing in Publication

Coles, Dudley, 1926-

  Leap of faith: a reflection on choices that shaped an extraordinary life / Dudley Coles.

ISBN 978-0-9810817-0-0

  1. Coles, Dudley, 1926- . 2. Salvation Army. 3. Salvationists--Canada--Biography. I. Title.

BX9743.C56A3 2008        287.9'6092        C2008-905568-3

To order additional copies or to contact the author,
please visit: www.colespublishing.com

# CONTENTS

| | |
|---|---|
| Acknowledgements | ix |
| Foreword | xi |
| Introduction | xiii |
| A Restless Ex-Serviceman | 1 |
|     Trying to Settle Down | 1 |
|     Eventful Days in isolated Berlin | 2 |
|     Scary moments in the Russian Zone | 3 |
| The Pivotal Point: 1949 - 1959 | 7 |
|     An Unsettled Beginning in Canada | 7 |
|     Interlude in London | 11 |
|     Preparation for Ministry | 12 |
|     Five Years, Three Corps – And a Wife! | 16 |
| Along The India Road | 25 |
|     Out of the Blue | 25 |
|     A Difficult Start | 29 |
|     In Journeys Most Frequent | 34 |
|     Happy to be Home | 39 |
| The India Road Continues | 47 |
|     Off to Hill School | 47 |
|     Holidays in the Hills | 53 |
|     Bombay Beckons | 59 |
|     Town of Joy | 65 |
|     Anand Central Corps | 69 |
| Publishing – For Goodness Sake | 73 |
|     A Last Sea Voyage | 73 |
|     The Joy of Writing | 74 |
|     Temporary Criminal Court Assignment | 75 |
|     Criminal Court Diary | 75 |

| | |
|---|---|
| Witnessing Without Words | 78 |
| The Weariness and Wonder of Words | 80 |
| An Unexpected Visitor | 84 |
| Facing Personal Challenges | 86 |
| **Blemished Pearl of the Orient** | **93** |
| The Trauma of Change | 93 |
| An Inauspicious Beginning | 96 |
| Getting on with Life Amid the Strife | 105 |
| **A Full Cup in London** | **111** |
| Roles and Goals | 111 |
| The Burden of Leadership | 118 |
| Dealing with Distresses | 123 |
| An Army of Disciplined Flexibility | 127 |
| **A Decade Of Consequences** | **131** |
| Blessings Beyond our Deserving | 131 |
| Return to Canada | 132 |
| The 'Write' Role for Me | 133 |
| Community Involvements | 134 |
| Recreational Pleasures | 136 |
| Time to Look Back | 138 |
| **A Goodly Heritage** | **141** |
| A New Century Dawns | 141 |
| Shy Young Man – Winsome Lass | 143 |
| A Marriage Made in Heaven | 147 |
| **A Teenager in Momentous Days** | **151** |
| Early Excitement and Adventure | 151 |
| A Boy in Wartime England | 154 |
| Wartime Service in the Royal Navy | 158 |
| Much to Ponder | 163 |
| **Conclusion** | **165** |

# CHOICES

*Is choice a tragedy?*

*It seems to me*
*It very often is.*
*But must it be?*
*Would it be better*
*If I couldn't choose?*

*Lord, in your mercy*
*Teach me how to use*
*The precious power*
*You dangerously give*
*To choose the way I work,*
*The way I live.*

*I don't ask you*
*To take my gift away,*
*But to guide me in my choices,*
*Every day!*
   ~ *John Gowans*

## DESTINY OF SHIPS AND MEN

*A ship can lie alongside a dock.*
   *But that is not what ships are for.*
*A ship can hug the coastline and ensure its safety and comfort.*
   *But that is rarely what ships are for.*
*A ship can head out into the deeps,*
   *Take some risks and fulfil its true destiny.*

~ *A.U.*

## ACKNOWLEDGEMENTS

The publication of this book brings to an end a long and perhaps too leisurely writing journey. Many friends have given advice or assistance along the way.

Notably I am grateful for the critiques and comments of Ray Wiseman (Fergus, Ontario), The Word Guild 2007 Canada Non-Fiction Best New Author Contest judges Gilbert G. Brandt and Elma Schemenauer, and Marina H. Hofman (Castle Quay Books). Salvation Army literary luminary Colonel Henry Gariepy (U.S.A.), and Major Charles King (current editor-in-chief and literary secretary at International Headquarters, London) have also read the manuscript and offered constructive comment.

I am greatly indebted to Lieut.-Colonel Maxwell Ryan for his final, meticulous manuscript reading, and to Nancy deLeeuw for her spectacular design skills so evident in the book covers. Volumes Publishing Ltd. must also be recognized for commendable efficiency and cooperation in the printing and publishing process.

Finally, my family. Proudly I recognize the immense help of our children, Heather, Howard and Graham whose computer, graphics and printing skills have been called upon many times, and for the wise counsel they, and their spouses (Michael, Cheryl and Julie), have given as we moved into publication mode. Lastly, how can I adequately thank Evangeline, my wife, for her thoughtful assessments, proof-reading of innumerable rewrites and unwavering encouragement throughout the long journey. I think God's blessing on *Leap of Faith* as it fulfils its own destiny in the coming days will be enough.

## Foreword

"What a series of rediscoveries life is," wrote C.S. Lewis on one occasion. Reading this life story of Dudley Coles is certainly like that. We rediscover through these fascinating chapters the key issues of living a life devoted to God and committed to serving humankind.

From the perspective of his retirement years, he has reflected on his life journey through several continents in the service of God within The Salvation Army. He has also been aided by his well-kept diaries. And it turns out for the reader to be a thrilling, inspiring and deeply human story.

Rather than a chronological autobiography, the author chooses to take us directly to post-war years when, as a World War II veteran, his restlessness leads through rare experiences before finding resolution in Toronto. After core chapters describing his faith adventures as a Salvation Army officer with his wife Evangeline, Dudley ponders the influence of heritage and environment in making significant life choices. He takes us back to his own pioneer Salvationist grandparents, his childhood in the family of the esteemed Colonel Bramwell Coles, his teen years in wartime England, and service on a British warship, to reach a convincing conclusion.

We are indebted to him for sharing his experiences, his faith and his philosophy in such a captivating way. Whether in territorial or international leadership roles, or learning to live in an Eastern culture, or discovering the arts of editorship, or struggling with his call to ministry, we watch his spiritual, intellectual and leadership development, and see the pre-eminence of spiritual values above material things. We glimpse a heart possessed by a conviction that a life lived for others is the most rewarding.

His frank comments reveal a man of insight, but he is also gifted with a great sense of humour that enables him to ride out many a frustrating experience.

Through it all, we see that Jesus Christ and service for him has been the mainstream of his life, and Dudley Coles emerges from these pages as a warm human being, a dedicated and thoughtful Salvation Army officer, a caring family man, and, I must add, a very fine writer.

*Eva Burrows*
*General (Retired)*

# INTRODUCTION

The culture and environment of our birth will undoubtedly have an enormous influence in setting up the stage upon which our life experience plays out. So will genetic endowments and predispositions.

Life is not pre-determined. We are not pawns on a chessboard. Luck does not shape our destiny and fate. Certainly, though, nature (genes) and nurture (environment) will affect the degree of struggle necessary to fulfill certain roles and ambitions.

As individuals with unique personalities and backgrounds, we will have opportunity to make choices that shape the meaning and value of our lives. And when we allow God to give direction and empowerment to the journey, we experience individual mission and purpose. This positively affects our choices, happiness and fulfillment.

Consider then the importance of choices. My son Graham reminded me rather sharply in early retirement how choices I made in the yesterdays of life powerfully influence choices I make today. We were talking about our retirement home.

There was much to commend the apartment in which we first lived on retirement. But it was a little short on space, and I had been quietly looking at condominiums. When we found a condominium with all that we could want in location, space and convenience I arranged a family get-together to seek endorsement.

To my chagrin the children and their spouses, and even my wife, Evangeline, left me in no doubt that the mortgage being talked about was beyond our means. "You don't want unnecessary stress at this time of life," said Howard. "Dad, we'd love you to own your own house," said Heather, "but at this point in life you would be taking too many risks." "And remember," said Graham with a knock-out blow, "you made choices early in life which limit your lifestyle now. Do you regret that?"

Do I regret that? A thousand times 'no!' Nothing could be more valued than our varied, exciting and challenging life experience. It's great to know that if we had the opportunity we would do it all over again, only a little better.

Our friends urge us to share these memories which are more than a little bit of family heritage to pass on to future generations. Primarily they reveal the deeply-held, God-guided motivations which brought to the life of Dudley and Evangeline Coles an unfailing sense of stability and meaning. Many memories also give the inner assurance of having made a difference for good in this wonderful but confused, sinful and needy world. What more could be desired?

The perimeters of this autobiography match those of the 20th Century. This helps me to set the boundaries and background of my life journey. Actually, I lived through three-quarters of the century. Some reference to the first 25 years of the 1900s will allow me to comment on significant aspects of my heritage—my parents and grandparents, and the world in which they lived. Nine years of retirement are also included to bring my story to the year 2000.

Readers may wonder, however, why I choose to begin this life story recollecting adventurous days on the Berlin Airlift (1948/1949), soon after my 22nd birthday. Why, too, do I conclude by recording adventurous World War II years, and service in the Royal Navy?

As this manuscript developed I found it of absorbing interest to note the importance of crucial choices and decisions, all through the journey of life. Choices are a central theme of my reminiscences. Significant choices, for which I am responsible, do not really begin until after my compulsory wartime service in the Armed Forces. It is at this point that restlessness begins, and I make my first consequential decisions. This is a good point to begin my life story. Only after I have reached retirement years do I return to my beginnings and measure the influence of heritage and early family life in the choices of mature years.

With the hindsight of retirement years also, I conclude each chapter with reflections on that segment of life's journey.

~~~ ~~~ ~~~

A few words are justified about The Salvation Army, as this distinctive segment of the Christian Church enormously provides the backdrop for the canvas of my life.

Historically, the autobiography provides an authentic ground-level view of The Salvation Army's distinctive and divinely-blessed ministry through a colourful and remarkable era of its short history—the 20$^{th}$ Century. Many good friends of the Army today have more admiration than understanding of this part of the Church. Usually it is simply known for its uniforms, bands and strong social conscience or, frequently, thrift stores and Christmas kettles. The chapters which follow may help people better to understand the Movement through which we have been given immeasurable opportunities for world-wide ministry in God's name.

In 1865 at Mile End Waste, London, England, the Rev. William Booth began outdoor street and tent meetings. These led to his leadership of the Christian Revival Association, later to become the Christian Mission. In 1878 the Movement became The Salvation Army, took on a quasi-military style—clearly suited to the spirit of the day—and Booth became its first General. Before he died in 1912, the Army had established its work in 58 countries.

Booth's passion to win the hearts and souls of people for Christ can never be doubted. Nor can his fiery spirit, his zealous evangelism and his concern for the needy. He was a spiritual parallel to Wellington and Napoleon in personal charisma and demonstrated leadership. When William Booth died, 65,000 grief-stricken people passed the coffin and 35,000 attended a memorial service. The heart of London stood still for nearly four hours as the lengthy funeral cortege wound its way through the city streets. It required three thousand policemen to control the crowds.

Nevertheless, William Booth would quickly acknowledge that he could never have fulfilled his great life's work without Catherine, his wife. Her keen intellect, her maturity, her level-headed support all balanced his mercurial spirit. Catherine, a great teacher and preacher, addressed public meetings throughout Britain with far-reaching results, despite lifelong frailty and ill-health. Now called 'the Army Mother', Catherine had an enormous influence on founding principles of the Movement, particularly in the doctrine of holiness (better understood today as incarnational Christian living), and in gender equality in ministry.

With those brief explanations we now jump forward to the late 1940s. By that time the Salvation Army had expanded to 104 countries and 160 languages. More than a million members worshipped in 15,000 churches and missions. More than 25,000 officers (pastors) and 800,000 employees administered its multi-faceted church and spiritually-focused humanitarian programs.

# CHAPTER 1: 1946 - 1949

## A RESTLESS EX-SERVICEMAN

### *Trying to Settle Down*

I think the restlessness begins immediately after World War II, and my discharge from the Royal Navy.

Canada House in London (with Norman Robertson as High Commissioner) negotiates with the Admiralty for my quick return from military service, so I can be given a new confidential assignment. All correspondence in the High Commissioner's office is handled through a central registry, and I am given responsibility for the care of all 'top secret' files.

It is good to be 'demobbed,' and back in an environment I thoroughly enjoy. Trafalgar Square is in the centre of London and, at lunch times, I enjoy immensely my walks around St. James's Park, or through Admiralty Arch to Buckingham Palace. Or up Charing Cross Road and The Strand, or down Whitehall to the Parliament buildings, Big Ben and Westminster Abbey. I always feel a sense of pride, too, as I walk up the imposing marble stairs into Canada House, acknowledged by the red-coated R.C.M.P. constable on duty.

But somehow, as a 19-year-old ex-serviceman, there is a restlessness that such a congenial environment hardly justifies. I believe there are limited career opportunities at Canada House, while in the newly-burgeoning airlines, the sky is the limit! Northolt Airport, near Harrow where I live, has become the home of British European Airways (later absorbed into British Airways), and here I am offered employment in the statistics section. The rapidly developing airline industry has its own excitement as almost daily new aircraft come into service and airport facilities expand. I regularly visit Heathrow (the home of British Overseas Airways Corporation) where most of the buildings are scattered Nissan huts left over from wartime use.

## Eventful Days in isolated Berlin

I have only been working for B.E.A. a year or so when an opportunity comes for my life to become a little more adventurous. In August 1948, the Russians suddenly close all road and rail links between Berlin and the West. Berlin, more than 100 miles inside the Russian Zone of Germany, is a divided city, with sectors being controlled by American, French and British, as well as Russian, occupying forces. To maintain the Western presence in Berlin and avoid being squeezed out of the former capital of Germany, the British and Americans begin an airlift of desperately needed supplies to their beleaguered sectors. It is soon apparent that more aircraft are required. B.E.A. is asked to organize a civil component of the Airlift, and to charter aircraft able to carry specialized loads. A statistical person is required for the small administrative staff set up at Gatow Airfield in Berlin. I am soon on my way! The B.E.A. staff are given honorary R.A.F. officer-status, and share their living quarters and amenities.

There are many teething troubles over the first few months as herculean efforts are made to bring efficiency and reliability to our part of this great undertaking. All aircraft must fly through a narrow air corridor into Berlin, and arrive at the Fronhau beacon within 30 seconds of scheduled time or return to base, such is the precise and tight integration of military and civil flights, 24 hours a day. Our difficulties compound because we are dealing with 23 charter companies and 103 aircraft. The aircraft—from Dakota to

Lancastrian, and Halton (Halifax) to York—vary greatly in speed, payloads and equipment. During the year before road and rail links are opened again, the civil airlift flies 21,921 successful sorties into Berlin, and carries 114,980 tons of life sustaining supplies. But at a cost of 21 lives.

While in Berlin I always try to visit Salvation Army corps on Sundays. All the Salvation Army work in East Berlin and East Germany is still disbanded, and the Army buildings (including territorial headquarters) requisitioned. In Western Berlin though, as well as in Allied Zones, brave efforts are made to recommence Salvationist activities. It is always a moving experience for me to share in a meeting in the quarters of two women officers whose corps building has been demolished. One half of the little group of worshippers, sit in the living room, and cannot see the other half in the dining room. But we can all see the meeting leader in the doorway between the two rooms. We sing with deep feeling borne of harsh experience, "Gestern, heute unt fur immer..."—Yesterday, today, forever—Jesus is the same! I also have association with one of the Salvation Army's post-war relief teams enormously involved with refugee and rehabilitation problems. Once I accompany the team to a former concentration camp—a sad memory.

### *Scary moments in the Russian Zone*

The Salvation Army has a canteen and recreation centre for military personnel in Berlin. For me these are enjoyable places to relax in a home-like atmosphere. I am invited to join some Salvationist servicemen-musicians on a weekend trip to Hanover, just after the road corridor has been re-opened. Can I forget that journey? We crowd into the back of a Red Shield truck and at the British checkpoint are given some security instructions regarding our journey through the Russian Zone. Relations between the Allies and Russians are still edgy. A short distance on we arrive at the Russian checkpoint where our travel documents are checked before we can proceed.

Once we are out of Berlin's suburbs and in the comparative safety of country surroundings, our German employee-driver stops the vehicle and opens a large wicker basket in the middle of the floor where we are sitting. To our unbelieving eyes, out from under some sheets jumps a young girl of about 20 who the driver immediately escorts to the front cab of the truck. She is an East German, and apparently our German driver is helping her to escape. Obviously, the driver knows the route, and two hours later he stops again at a quiet place on the road. The young woman climbs back into the basket and is quickly hidden under the sheets.

Soon we are at the Helmstedt checkpoint near Hanover, and instructed to go into the Russian control point office. There an officer examines our documentation again, and asks if we have anything in the truck that needs to be declared. We are in a dilemma. If we admit the girl's presence, she will face death, or harsh imprisonment at the least. But if we do not and she is found, we will also be seriously at risk. If a white lie is ever justified, perhaps it is in such a situation. We say, "No."

To our alarm, the officer sends a soldier to examine the truck, and through the windows of the office we watch as he pauses at the rear of the vehicle trying to decide whether to clamber aboard and examine the basket or not. Outwardly we try to chat nonchalantly, but inwardly our hearts are pounding. It seems like an eternity before the Soviet soldier decides not to bother, and moves around to the front cab. The relief we experience when we pass through the British checkpoint a little later on can be imagined! The young woman, with a shout of joy, and many "danke schon's," jumps down and disappears into a nearby crowd.

While in Berlin, I have to take regular pay-day flights out to Wunsdorf, a base for civil airlift flights in the British Zone. On one occasion my return trip coincides with the departure of a British South America Airways Tudor aircraft captained by a British Salvationist friend, Bernard Patrick. He invites me to fly out with him. Two large tanks in the stripped fuselage carry more than 2,000 gallons of diesel fuel. Once we have cleared the Wunsdorf air controllers and are safely into our slot on the corridor bound for Berlin, my pilot friend switches over to the BBC in London. To our great surprise we are listening to a Salvation Army band playing music, which brings nostalgic memories to us both. These serendipitous moments are soon interrupted, however, as Bernard switches over to Berlin flight controllers who will guide us into Gatow.

Soon after this, the B.E.A. civil airlift staff is transferred to Luneburg, in the Western Zone, where we join Headquarters, No.46 Group, R.A.F. The airfield is pleasantly quiet and peaceful compared to Gatow, and the town truly picturesque. It is lovely to hear the birds chirping as I wake each day, and to be surrounded by some of West Germany's rural beauty. In the officers' mess, one of the women who serves us with gracious dignity is the wife of the former German air force commander at Luneberg.

The airlift ends in August 1949, and I resume my employment with B.E.A. at Northolt, just a few miles from our Harrow home. I am 23 and it is time perhaps that I settle down, but the restlessness of youth now focused in a new direction. What about Canada?

Yes, I am a Canadian by birth, and had better check out my homeland before developing any serious attachments in England. Mother and Father raise no objections, and soon I am on board the *Queen Mary* bound for New York, followed by a short train journey to Toronto. Ship journeys seem to mark out important watershed points in my life, and this voyage is no exception.

## *REFLECTIONS*

It is interesting to reflect on the decisions made as a young man.  Life is opening up for me, with limitless possibilities.  What road shall I take?  My initial entry back into civilian life is made easy by the offer of an early Navy discharge if I return to Canada House.  But soon other opportunities beckon, and the choice to 'check out Canada' is my first decision of lifetime consequence.

## CHAPTER 2

## THE PIVOTAL POINT: 1949 - 1959

### *An Unsettled Beginning in Canada*

It is an unsettled young man who crosses the Atlantic Ocean on board the *Queen Mary* in 1949. I am not depressed, but simply unsure about the future. The war years and immediate post-war years in England are now behind me. I am keen to get acquainted again with the land of my birth, Canada. Does my future lie here?

Actually, the war separates the Coles family forever. Gordon, my eldest brother, is called up immediately for military service, and soon other siblings follow. We never live as a complete family in our parental home again. Gordon and Bramwell, after 'demob.', quickly marry and, discouraged with the housing problems in England, emigrate with their spouses, Pat and Dorothy, to Canada. They settle in Toronto. Likewise Joan, after Salvation Army officer-training in London, is transferred to Toronto and an eagerly-awaited marriage of childhood sweethearts follows. Raymond, a year younger than me, returns to Canada with the Canadian military which he has joined in England after training in the British Army.

So it is probably the pull of family already in Canada, together with my own happy recollections of childhood years, that beckons me to the land of the Maple Leaf. Inner excitement mounts as the train taking me from New York approaches Toronto's Union Station. What lies ahead for me behind the curtain of the unknown tomorrow?

Bram and Dorothy, who are already looking after Ray, gladly take in another 'boarder.' My clearest memory is of sharing our meagre financial resources to purchase a car, a Hillman. Unfortunately, I am the last one to learn to drive and the first to have an accident! The car is a write-off but Ray, always the entrepreneurial type, soon has us sharing an upscale Hillman Humber Hawk. How we manage to share one car equitably and happily I don't know!

My first priority is to look for work. As a result of airline recommendations given to me in England before departure, I am flown by Trans Canada Airlines to Montreal and offered a job with them or with the International Civil Aviation Organization—both, however, in Montreal. I am more comfortable about staying in Toronto and declined these superb offers.

After considering employment as a stenographer for the Canadian National Railways, I eventually commence work as a clerk in the Toronto Branch of British American Oil Company— later Gulf Oil Canada, and now Petro Canada. The branch is situated in a depressing area of the city near the Keating Street docks. Many of our trucks supply homeowners with domestic fuel in the winter, and we are contracted to keep their oil tanks from running dry. This is the prime means of home heating. One of our office responsibilities is to constantly update our estimate of when tanks will need refilling. This requires several mathematical calculations based on the date last filled, daily temperatures since that date, and the number of rooms in the home. Quite a chore, and not always successful!

I commence cost accounting studies, and soon am happily promoted to chief clerk. After passing intermediate exams, I transfer to B-A's head office accounting department in the more salubrious surroundings of Bay and College Streets. I recognize a number of other Salvationists who are holding responsible positions with B-A Oil.

Meanwhile I link up with the Salvation Army's Danforth Corps and become involved in its activities: senior band and songsters, teaching Sunday school classes and, eventually, taking over leadership of the young people's band. Life is good. Superficially I do not have a care in the world. But deep down there is a restlessness that cannot be quelled.

When a first little baby is expected at the Bram and Dorothy Coles homestead, Ray and I move to a boarding house in downtown Toronto. Our landlord-hostess always packs mammoth corned beef sandwiches for our weekday lunches. Hearty evening meals are shared around the large dining room table with a dozen boarders under the commanding supervision of our hostess. Her warm heart matches her ample proportions. Later, however, I eagerly respond to the invitation of a fine Salvationist couple of Danforth Corps to board with them. This proves even more congenial, and is only terminated by the natural pull of a parental home once again when mother and father settle in Toronto on retirement in late 1952.

Though life is good, inner restlessness persists and has to be resolved. "The Hound of Heaven,"—whose pursuit of man's soul is so eloquently described in Francis Thompson's famous poem (and musically portrayed in one of my father's band compositions, *Divine Pursuit*) encapsulates my feelings:

> *I fled Him, down the nights and down the days;*
> *I fled Him, down the arches of the years;*
> *I fled Him, down the labyrinthine ways*
> *Of my own mind; and in the mist of tears...*
>
> *From those strong Feet that followed,*
> *Followed after,*
> *But with unhurrying chase,*
> *And unperturbed pace,*
> *Deliberate speed, majestic instancy,*

*They beat—and a voice beat
More instant than the Feet—
"All things betray thee, who betrayest Me."*

God is following me with unfaltering step and gentle persistence. Quite simply He is calling me to be a Salvation Army officer. I am tenaciously resisting the idea.

Of course, the longer I try to avoid the great decision, the more complicated life becomes. There are two obstacles. Firstly, I have a slight stammer. Its origins seemed to stem from my earliest school days when I was compelled to write with my right hand, though naturally a 'lefty'. Surely this will be an obvious hindrance to public ministry. Secondly, I have a girl friend who cannot understand my inward struggle. I am very fond of her.

Then dawns a day never to be forgotten. The pivotal point around which my future life is to revolve. It is the evening of February 22, 1953, and I decide to go with my father (it is his birthday) to North Toronto Corps. Commissioner William Dalziel is conducting weekend celebrations marking the opening of the attractively renovated and greatly enhanced corps building.

I am in spiritual turmoil throughout the meeting. All details are forgotten except a verse of George Matheson's haunting hymn, sung just before the benediction:
*"O Love that wilt not let me go,
I rest my weary soul in Thee,
I give Thee back the life I owe,
That in Thine ocean depths its flow
May richer, fuller be."*

The words are like an electric shock to my system. They are the prayer God longs to hear me make to Him. Compelled by an unseen Hand, I stand up and walk to the place of prayer, the Mercy Seat. With anguished heart and a flood of tears I surrender my life unconditionally. God is calling me to a life of spiritual ministry as an officer of The Salvation Army.

Leaving the building that night there is peace in my heart, but still much mental turmoil. I cannot stop the tears as I think of the immediate consequences of my commitment. Father decides it will be better for us to walk home rather than take the streetcar! Kind parents help me through the difficult days that follow, as do the understanding parents of a girl friend who is as heart-broken as I am.

## *Interlude in London*

To help set a new direction for my life I decide to quit work and spend three months in England prior to entering the Salvation Army training college in Toronto. I have relatives and friends in England, and a kind aunt and uncle living at Staines near London offer me accommodation.

On arrival I have the good fortune to be offered a temporary job at Canada House (a former place of employment), on the High Commissioner's special Coronation staff. The crowning of Queen Elizabeth II at Westminster Abbey and the processional to and from Buckingham Palace are events of breathtaking pomp and pageantry. Many Canadians look to Canada House to arrange seating for these events as well as other hospitality courtesies.

I have the privilege of seeing the coronation procession from the stands built outside Canada House, as the parade passes through Trafalgar Square no fewer than three times. This is one of the best positions on the whole route.

The weather on that early June day in 1953 could hardly have been less kind. It is wet, cold and miserable. But thousands of people packing the square below us seem undeterred, and an air of expectancy mounts following our 6:00 a.m. seating deadline.

Right from the colonial contingents (as they were called in those days) that head the procession, to the brilliantly-plumed Household Cavalry that escort the great, golden state coach, the spectacular colour, magnitude and magnificence of the cavalcade is awesome. I do not suppose that ever again will we see so many royal personages, prime ministers, top service chiefs and leading representatives of so many countries in a single procession.

In startling but happy contrast, I am cycling in the vast expanse of Windsor Great Park a few weeks later with my aunt and uncle. They take me to Duke's Drive, a place known to few but local inhabitants. It is Ascot week and at this point the Queen and Royal Family transfer from their cars, which have brought them from Windsor Castle, into imposing state landaus drawn by the famous Windsor Greys.

This takes ten minutes and it is a rare experience to watch at close hand as the Queen and her party transfer. Then, with colourful escorts, they move gently off down the winding drive under a canopy of trees to make their state entry into Ascot.

Another rare happenstance follows a little later as, rounding a bend in a wooded area of the park, we almost collide with a little boy, his sister and three adults. I can hardly believe my eyes, for I have almost run down Prince Charles and Princess Anne, out for a walk with their matron, a nurse and detective.

### *Preparation for Ministry*

It is with some outward trepidation but strong inner conviction that I arrive at the Salvation Army's training college, then situated at 84 Davisville Avenue in Toronto, and only a mile from my home. All my possessions are in a trunk, a suitcase and a box.

The Shepherds' Session of cadets comprises 67 cadets; 41 single women, 18 single men and just four married couples. At 27 I am one of the older cadets, the average age of the session being 21-and-a-half. My brother Raymond and his wife Catherine are Shepherds, too.

Establishing a student council is an innovative idea of our new principal, Brigadier Wesley Rich, a British officer whose most recent appointment had been in the U.S.A. I am elected the council's first president, and at Christmas time a new secretary is elected. Her name is Evangeline Oxbury. Her winsome smile and happy laughter immediately captivate my attention and interest. She is petite and attractive.

There is little opportunity, and less encouragement, to get involved in romances during training! Men and women are kept severely apart, with separate dining rooms and different half-days off. In the lecture hall and classrooms we sit on opposite sides—there is always a great divide.

Such restrictions are only challenges to adventurous response, as eight cadets now married to session-mates can testify! In my own case there are three special situations that enhance contact and prospects. The first, of course, results from the necessary duties of a student council president and secretary. Even the officer designated to oversight all council activities has to allow some extra 'business' fraternization.

Then there is the matter of work-sections! At one point in the session, Cadet Oxbury is given the assignment of the principal's office. By strange co-incidence, and shortly thereafter, another cadet and I decide we need a change. We make our own private work section swap. By another serendipitous happenstance, Cadet Eva Oxbury soon finds that she is polishing the inside brass door-knob of the principal's office as another cadet (not to be named!) is polishing the outside door-knob.

But most surprising—and helpful—is the match-making concern of Brigadier and Mrs. Rich themselves. Just before the end of the session I am asked by the principal if there is anyone in the session I might be interested in. Our first appointments are being prepared, and an effort can be made to see we are not more than a few hundred miles apart. Canada is a big country!

Flabbergasted, I reply, "Naturally I'm looking around, but I haven't made any serious approaches to anyone. Within the college rules, how can I know that any feelings I might have toward a woman cadet are reciprocated?"

"Well, if you can tell me who that might be, an arrangement could be made for the two of you to meet somewhere off the college grounds within the next week to find out."

Sufficient to say that we do meet briefly. Cadet Oxbury (we never think of using first names) agrees to meet me at a nearby park. During our short tete-a-tete, I quote Romans 8:28, "All things work together for good to them that love God..." Immediately Eva takes a text from her pocket. She had just taken it from her promise box before she left the college to give to me. It is Romans 8:28!

"Oh," I say with palpitating heart, "I must ask God to give me a sign, too, through a promise box." The opportunity comes a week or two later when my cadet brigade is visiting a Montreal corps. At supper time, my host and hostess pass around a promise box. I pick and read John 13:34: "A new commandment I give unto you, That ye love one another..." Can I believe my eyes? Dare I argue?

Cadets have little time to get into trouble. Our nine-month session is crowded with lectures, Bible and doctrine studies, and practical community evangelism. We study in our little cubicles, or down in our trunk rooms, early in the morning and late at night. The four married couples are not allowed to bring their children with them to the college, so no time is set aside for family affairs. We consider our musical activities, particularly band and singing groups, as relaxing times on our schedule. Ray and I are proud that the music for our sessional song is written by Colonel Bramwell Coles (R), and father comes to the college on several occasions to teach us the song. It is difficult to sing well but has a message that grips us all.

The monthly spiritual days led by leaders of the territory always seem more 'holy' than Sundays, and conclude with many of us making deeper commitments to match a deeper understanding of God's will and Word. Our disciplined training regime also includes classes in church and Salvation Army history, public speaking, sermon preparation, and Orders and Regulations. 'O. & R.', which covers every subject from hair tidiness to rules for visitation, from loyalty and obedience to relationships prior to marriage, is a distillation of the wisdom of the years, and aids the Army's international unity and identity.

Occasionally we cause our over-worked staff—sometimes under great strain—trouble they little deserve. There is the memory, for instance, of an early morning hour when all the men cadets are instructed to gather in a classroom. An atmosphere of foreboding and crisis prevails. We stand in stunned silence for 20 minutes as the side officer gives us a verbal lashing. We are left in no doubt that because of unnamed activities the previous evening, we will be remembered as one of the most disappointing sessions in training history. The lecture continues until one married cadet with impressive boldness interrupts the passionate monologue to ask: "Excuse me, sir, but what makes you think it is the male cadets?" The good side officer's blood pressure must have risen several notches more when he discovers he is speaking to the wrong group. It is the women cadets who sent his two sons to buy hamburgers with the admonition, "Don't tell your dad!"

Just before the end of the session the territorial commander, shortly to retire, visits the college to share a celebration. He is completing 50 years as an officer. His informal talk, "Ten things life has taught me" is impressive. I even jot all the headings down. It is something of a let down a few months later, though, when I discover the same ten points are in a book of 2,000 sermon illustrations under the slightly altered heading—Ten things life should teach you!

A natural high point of our commissioning weekend at Toronto's familiar Salvationist mecca, Massey Hall, comes in concluding moments. With eager anticipation we receive our first appointments as probationary lieutenants of The Salvation Army. I am appointed to Pembroke, Ontario. A lone but loud 'hallelujah' reverberates from the back of the top gallery. It is my new commanding officer, 1$^{st}$ Lieutenant Roy Calvert (ultimately to become territorial commander). Cadet Evangeline Oxbury is appointed to Orangeville, Ontario—too far for me to visit in one day. But then, we still don't have permission for "official correspondence." That will have to await 'evidence of effective service for God and the Army.' However, there is excitement and happiness that night as we travel back to the college together, and exchange our first gentle kisses.

### *Five Years, Three Corps – And a Wife!*

Five eventful years on the 'field' in Canada begin with Roy Calvert kindly picking me up in his old jalopy to take me to Pembroke. I think he is keen to have someone who could push if necessary. But without incident we jogged up No.11 highway to Huntsville, through Algonquin Park and then into the Ottawa Valley and Pembroke. Our only problem is the lateness of our arrival, and the need to find a hotel for what remains of the night. Roy could have chosen better!

Most newly-commisioned officers are still single and it is common for us to be paired together. Roy and I get along well, though my cooking leaves something to be desired. I spent most of one Saturday morning making a lemon meringue pie, just to show my C.O. what a remarkable assistant he has. I am busy about other tasks when the smell of burning fills the house. I reach the oven in time to see the last remains of my morning labours as burning embers.

Shortly after arrival I am instructed to assist at the divisional youth camp at Lac Lachigan, Quebec. Every summer a Log Book is dug up from under a tree at the beginning of the camping season, and the previous year's record read out. Then new records are added of the current summer's activities. At season's end the book is carefully wrapped and again buried in a closing ceremony marked by appropriate pomp and circumstance. Later that night, a fellow "Shepherd," Ralph Godfrey, and I creep out and dig up the log book, replacing it with a little note— "Ha, ha, fooled you! Look under one of the other trees!" I never did hear what happened the next year, because I also have a surprise—I am to be moved!

Roy is really to blame. It happens when the Field Secretary (Colonel Clarence Wiseman) visits our division. He arrives in Pembroke one weekday to conduct a meeting. In a moment of not unnatural generosity, Roy suggests to him that Dudley Coles is not really a 'young' lieutenant, and ought to be in charge of his own corps. To the Field Secretary who happens to be trying to resolve a corps (church) leadership problem at that moment, this news undoubtedly comes as manna from heaven. Within a few weeks I have farewelled from Pembroke and arrive at East Windsor (originally Ford City Outpost), alone and in charge.

It is challenging to have my own little congregation. With more enthusiasm than wisdom, perhaps, I set about turning the corps upside down to make it a 'hot-bed of salvationism.' The motto 'Every soldier an active soldier' is adopted, quarterly activity schedules are prepared, and the involvement of every soldier is taken for granted. Amazingly, the warm-hearted people overlook the failings of their inexperienced lieutenant and give him fantastic support. He soon has a *War Cry* brigade' of 14 who help him visit 17 taverns in the district every weekend with the Army's flagship paper. We also visit a number of institutions, and perimeter communities assigned to East Windsor.

Further progress is assured with the arrival of Envoy William Clarke in the district. Quickly he is appointed corps sergeant major, and brings his many gifts and unfaltering support to every phase of corps activity.

Meanwhile, a private agenda must be pursued with equal tenacity and enthusiasm. The agenda has one item—Lieutenant Evangeline Oxbury! The Lieutenant has been transferred from Orangeville to Goderich, where she is now in charge. The rules allow me to see her one day a month, and five of those hours are taken up travelling.

A highlight is the summer holiday train trip across Canada with Eva to meet her parents in Powell River, B.C. Travelling has always held a fascination for me, and the Canadian Pacific Railway's 'Canadian' with its two scenic domes and rear lounge car, as well as dining cars and snack areas provides a great setting for viewing the contrasting landscapes of our great country.

Excitement mounts on this first Western jaunt as, on reaching Vancouver, we begin the last 100 miles of our four-day journey. The winding gravel road to Powell River has only just been opened, and the route across the undulating Sechelt Peninsula includes two ferry crossings of immense beauty.

Eva's parents and family greet me warmly. Naturally I am especially pleased to meet them, and to relax in the lovely atmosphere of their home and surroundings. I am awed by the breath-taking view of ocean, lakes and mountains, and the paper mill town itself, all of which have had such an influence on Eva's early years.

I am a little scared about approaching Eva's dad, Roland Oxbury, about marriage to his daughter. Two years earlier he had been chosen Powell River's good citizen of the year. But, super gentleman that he is, he gives his consent willingly. He is very proud of Eva. In a poignant letter handed to her as she left home for the training college Dad Oxbury says that she is doing what he ought to have done thirty years earlier!

When we return to Ontario, Eva moves into her new appointment as commanding officer at Goderich, on Lake Huron. While this is not as far as Orangeville for me to travel for the one-day-a-month visit, we still do not relish the further year of waiting stipulated by *Orders and Regulations for Salvation Army Officers*. It requires of us considerable diplomatic correspondence, coupled with the completion of all post-training studies, and continued success at East Windsor and Goderich respectively. Finally a somewhat reluctant higher authority is able to give permission for a January 1956 wedding—six months early!

I had always enjoyed my bachelor days, but all my brothers and my sister are now well and truly married, and I am almost thirty. The little lieutenant from B.C. had taken away the glamour of bachelorhood. Our wedding takes place at North Toronto Citadel on a Friday evening in January—the only time slot available that month.

Unforgotten are my mother's words at the reception. I still have some of her notes. She remembers looking at us all and wondering what we would become in mature years. "The boys had a great idea of keeping a big store which sold everything, 'Coles Brothers Limited.' Father and I would get everything free. Dudley said, 'And you can help yourself to a new dress whenever you want.' Well I still have to pay for everything, even dresses, but I would not want to change anything."

Mother also gives us some advice still vividly recalled. "Marriage is a living thing, and if it is to survive, it must be nurtured, carefully tended and treasured; otherwise it can become just a monotonous existence. Make sure it is built on unselfishness, thoughtfulness and staunch loyalty. Maximize the good things, and minimize the bad." This is good advice, and wiser than we can possibly realize at the time.

Salvationists at East Windsor welcome Eva as warmly as they had welcomed me 14 months earlier. In turn the new Mrs. Lieutenant Coles brings a stronger dimension of caring and enthusiasm to our united ministry.

Since its 19<sup>th</sup> century beginnings, The Salvation Army has believed in "gender equality" in spiritual ministry. The equal training of men and women in Salvation Army training colleges, and the regulation that requires officer to marry officer, results in mutual absorption in the grand task of Kingdom building. Gender equality does not mean, however, that either partner pursues a self-centred career ambition to the detriment of the other. Their marriage service includes the commitment to constantly seek each other's good, and to ensure that the fruitfulness of their combined service is enhanced thereby.

Understandably it takes Eva and me a little while to adjust to all the implications of marriage. We hardly know each other at depth, and our lives in many ways have followed different paths. I am more obstinate than I realize, and too often assume that Eva will think and act like I do. To my great surprise there are one or two occasions when, in unbearable frustration, Eva just marches out of the quarters. I am scared, and do a lot of praying until in an hour or so she returns! We both apologize quickly, and life resumes its normal atmosphere of happy partnership and deepening love. Eva's feelings lie much closer to the surface than mine, but she never allows annoyance or disagreement to simmer for long. She has a special gift for adhering to the Scriptural injunction, "Never go to bed angry."

Hardly eighteen months after our marriage, and shortly after receiving "farewell orders," the sad news arrives from Powell River that Eva's brother, Ernie, has died of cancer. He is engaged to be married. We are given permission to fly to B.C. immediately, and take our furlough at the same time. Some hectic hours are first spent putting all our belongings in storage as the incoming officers are expected shortly. Ernie was a most likeable young man, kind and friendly, and I quickly share the sadness of his loss. While Mum and Dad Oxbury largely hide their feelings, the loss of Ernie who has so desperately clung to life, and the seeming failure of much prayer on his behalf, tests their faith severely.

Our own faith is tested even further by the new appointment given to us. We had hoped it would be nearer B.C., but instead it is to Kentville, Nova Scotia. Could we be much further from Eva's home? Little do we imagine what the future holds.

From Powell River, we travel by bus through the United States to Windsor, pick up our belongings and a new Volkeswagon and journey into Eastern Canada. Kentville, of course, is in the heart of the beautiful Annapolis Valley, and adjacent to historic Grand Pre and Wolfville—a lovely part of Canada.

We soon settle down to busy corps activities that include two sizeable outposts to care for. The Kentville corps building has recently been remodelled, and our quarters is a lovely house situated on the edge of town, at the top of the hill, and opposite the T.B. hospital.

Broadcasting is quite a challenging part of our new tasks. Once a month the Sunday evening meeting is aired for an hour. I vividly remember our first foray into this new field of witness. I carefully plan every moment of the meeting, like General Eisenhower planning for D-Day. Timing is meticulously watched, and I practise my sermon a dozen times in the bedroom. The momentous day arrives and all goes well until, at the conclusion of my sermon, I discover there is still 15 minutes of broadcasting time left. I launch into the prayer song, "Just As I Am," and after singing its six verses am horrified to discover there are still seven minutes of broadcasting time to fill. It is the longest seven minutes of my life, as with spontaneous comments and some further repeats of "Just As I Am," the hour is completed.

Another appreciated broadcasting opportunity is the "Children's Bible Hour," aired every Saturday morning. Eva and I carefully prepare for this, and find it an influential ministry. There is a dual radio station at Windsor, our neighbouring town, and one Saturday we arrange for Lieutenant Bramwell Tillsley in Windsor, and Lieutenant Ralph Stanley (visiting us from Dartmouth), to play a cornet duet—25 miles apart! It is quite an achievement, and enjoyed immensely by our Annapolis Valley listening audience.

Kentville will always be remembered as the birthplace of Heather. She is our first child, although there had been a miscarriage in Windsor. I remember Heather's birth clearly because, while I am not allowed anywhere near the delivery room, I do go out with the doctor on an emergency call. Midnight is approaching. Two teenagers, seriously hurt in a car accident out of town, are being flown in to a nearby ball park. Somehow I almost get swiped by the helicopter as it lands on the field. Sadly, while the doctor arranges for transfer of the girls to hospital, one dies. After I give some minor assistance, the doctor suggests I go home and have some sleep. He will phone me when there is some news.

I must admit to thinking more about the ballpark than the delivery room as I succumb to sleep in an early morning hour. Awakened by a 6:00 a.m. phone call, I am told that I am the father of a beautiful baby daughter who, with her mother, is doing fine. Mothers stay in hospital for five days to a week, and fathers are allowed to see their offspring only through a glass window of the nursery where they are held up momentarily by a duty nurse. But how proud I am!

Three months later, Heather Evangeline is dedicated by my brother-in-law and sister, Majors John and Joan Carter, then stationed at Moncton. Mother and Father also visit us during our Kentville stay, and their weekend includes a fine band program with Halifax Citadel Band (E.Elloway) and our little Kentville group under my leadership. After we make our long-rehearsed contributions, Father, always a diplomat, very kindly congratulates us on our "courage and enthusiasm"!

Another special memory of Kentville is the mine disaster at Springhill. As soon as I hear about it on the local radio I phone Captain George Heron (newly arrived at Windsor) and we decide to leave immediately to give assistance. It is a tragic accident in North America's deepest mine, and 74 men lose their lives. The atmosphere around the mine site is one of unbearable anxiety and tension as rescuers work frantically to reach the trapped men. What happiness and relief as a dozen men are brought to the surface after being entombed for six days!

We remain for almost a week, sharing in the Army's special refreshment and counselling assignments. The corps officers' house is a miniature Grand Central Station with officers sleeping and eating in shifts throughout the day and night.

We officers of Nova Scotia are then replaced so that we can travel to Halifax for the great Maritime congress gatherings to be conducted by Commissioner William Dray, chief of the staff.

What tremendous energy we must have in our youthful years! After a strenuous and emotionally-draining week at Springhill, I arrive at Halifax (with Eva, of course) to undertake the heaviest assignment ever given to me—that of reporting the four-day event for *The War Cry*. (I am already writing periodic feature columns for the *Cry* and the youth-oriented *Crest* magazine.)

The congress is a mammoth task, and gives little time for the usual "light-hearted moments of relaxation"—a fact noted by the divisional commander and the editor-in-chief in letters of appreciation. Father, with his own editorial facility and experience, is pleased that I have this assignment and, bless his heart, inundates me with all sorts of ideas and advice. Included in some vital opening paragraphs aimed at providing an "impressionistic review of things, and an air of importance to the events," he suggest I bring some local color, viz:

"Many of these Maritimers earn their livelihood by extracting wealth from the soil, from the depths of the earth and from the sea, and certain it is that during these congress days all Salvationists who are fortunate enough to be present at these gatherings, are likewise out to extract every ounce of spiritual wealth from the various events programmed."

While many of his ideas are incorporated into my report, this particular introductory paragraph is omitted. More desirable is a timely reference to the Springhill mine disaster, still deeply touching people's hearts and minds.

## ~ REFLECTIONS ~

The return to Canada is not an irrevocable decision. I have no commitments, attachments or obligations. I am free to open my life to new surroundings and opportunities, or return to England. I wonder now, though, what path my life might have taken had I accepted the airline offers in Montreal.

But it is in Toronto where the pivotal point is faced, and all other options set aside for the compelling call and challenge of God's service. At last I have found a focus, a leap of faith that narrows enormously future choices and decisions.

There is, though, one other choice of profound significance to the fulfilling of my God-shaped destiny. His hand is clearly evident in my marriage to Evangeline Oxbury. Two months before my 30$^{th}$ birthday two crucial choices and decisions have been made.

But life will have many more, even within the narrower focus of future days. One will come all too soon.

## CHAPTER 3: 1959 - 1964

## ALONG THE INDIA ROAD

### *Out of the Blue*

In spite of congress reporting deadlines we do have to nourish body as well as spirit. So Eva and I are happy to join my sister Joan and her husband John at an attractive Halifax restaurant on Canada's Atlantic seaboard. As we tuck into tempting ice cream sundaes, we discuss the great congress events just concluded.

In particular, we talk about the appeal for missionary reinforcements in an officers' council that afternoon. Between mouthfuls of the delicious refreshment Eva and I agree that we do not feel an irresistible 'call' to offer ourselves for overseas service immediately. Nevertheless, if we are asked 'out of the blue,' we would feel compelled to respond. (John and Joan do, in fact, make a positive response in writing to territorial headquarters.)

However, it all seems so remote and improbable that Eva and I do not give it another thought as we return to our delightful quarters at Kentville. Little do we dream that within three months we will be put to the test.

It is a crisp and snowy January day when the letter arrives. Eva is upstairs attending to the morning bath of our six-month old daughter, Heather. "Not much this morning," the postman cheerfully comments as he thrusts a solitary letter into my hand. Momentarily I agree with him, but quickly change my mind on glancing at the envelope. Why should territorial headquarters in

Toronto be sending a letter marked 'private' to a young lieutenant couple?

The staff secretary's first paragraph catches my breath. "I have been requested by the chief secretary to send you this confidential letter, and I can quite understand that its arrival will give you and Mrs. Coles cause for considerable thought..." I hurriedly scan the rest with increasing amazement and then, mind awhirl and heart a-flutter but trying to display outward calm, I take the letter upstairs to Evangeline. "Sit down a minute," I say. "Here comes the biggest shock you've ever had. We've been asked to go to Poona, India!"

Like many mothers, the first thing Eva does is to have a good cry! Then we make some coffee and begin to discuss the unbelievable request seriously. I immediately find a map and also a Salvation Army *Year Book* to discover what I can about the Poona appointment. The year book is cryptic but illuminating—

"*AUDIT AND 'WAR CRY' OFFICES, POONA*

This is the International Headquarters Audit Office for India, Pakistan, Burma and Ceylon; also the registered office of The Salvation Army in India as incorporated under the Indian Companies Act. The Poona office publishes a monthly English edition of *The War Cry* for the India territories, Pakistan, Burma and Ceylon. Statistics: officers 4."

Eva's initial tearful reaction is understandable. Throughout the five years since leaving training college, thousands of miles separated Eva from her West Coast home. Our first married appointment had been in Windsor, Ontario. When farewell orders were received there, we were sure—and assured—that our next appointment would be nearer Eva's home where a brother lay critically ill. Instead, our marching orders were to Kentville, a further 1,000 miles east. In an effort to console my young wife I got the not-so-bright idea of suggesting that (excluding

Newfoundland) Nova Scotia was just about the 'end of the line.' We couldn't possibly go further. Our next move was bound to take us closer to her native British Columbia.

I miscalculated. For now we are being asked to go half way round the world, 13,000 miles, and no possible appointment can take us further. Immediately we are tempted to allow the resolve made in the comfortable surroundings and congenial atmosphere of that Halifax restaurant to dissolve as quickly as the ice cream. However, after some hours of quiet discussion, we could not get away from the conviction that it is a great deal easier to do that which God has called us to do, no matter how difficult it is, than to face the responsibility of not doing it. Further, we were led to recall that in training college days there had been some indications that missionary service might be God's way for us. Could we doubt any longer?

That afternoon, letters are sent off to our parents seeking their reactions. "Our feelings are naturally mixed," we write. "We are not overly excited for we realize something of that which is involved. But we feel strongly that to do other than accept would limit God's control of our lives, and handicap our spiritual experience. Almost every week from our platform we preach that complete trust in God and obedience to His revealed will are necessary to spiritual growth and happiness. Now God is calling us in a greater way than ever before to prove that which we preach.

"Somehow we never really expected that a decision like this would be required of us, and now that it has come, it hardly seems true. But true it is, and all we can do is pray that special grace and spiritual resources shall be given us as we face all the implications of this decision..."

The immediate response from our homes is hardly encouraging. With natural love and concern, our parents doubt whether we know, or are prepared for, the hardship, sacrifice and adjustment necessary. Clearly anxious about our health and that of the new little life so recently entrusted to us they raise questions. Do we realize that our pay is much less, our standard of living lower? Did we understand that my work involves long absences from home, and that at the age of five, children are sent away to boarding schools for their education?

Of course they are right. We hardly grasp the costliness of our decision. But we have already sent a reply to the staff secretary saying that we will go for five years. Quickly we ask my parents in Toronto if they can stop the letter before it is opened. As we give the matter further thought and prayer, however, we clearly see the hand of God in it all. So when Mother phones back a day later with what she thinks is good news, we have to tell her the decision our more reflective thinking had led us to. There is a poignant silence at the other end of the phone, and then a quiet voice, "Alright dears, I will let headquarters know the letter can be opened." Further letters arriving from our homes bring joy and relief, striking a more positive note and assuring us of loving, prayerful support as we follow through our heart-wrenching decision.

One letter reads—"We cannot say that we are particularly pleased that you may be going so far away, but it is an understatement to say that we are exceedingly proud of you. Your letter explains a lot more reasons why you should go than we can find why you should not, and we believe that Christ will be the answer to your every need."

In a follow-up letter to territorial headquarters we conclude, "We pray that God will strengthen us for the decision we have made with all that it involves."

Much correspondence, innumerable injections, many interviews and endless packing occupy much of the next four months before we bid farewell to our loved ones, friends and

Canada. A long six weeks' journey east begins. We have the sensation of being filled simultaneously with trepidation and excitement. Though loathe to leave our homeland, we keenly anticipate the revolutionary experiences soon to be ours.

After long weeks of sea travel, we spy through the mist of a wet, dismal day the rain-shrouded coastline of India. Slowly, *R.M.S. Caledonia* approaches the Bombay waterfront with its famous Taj Mahal hotel and Gateway to India landmarks. Although Ballard Pier does not look especially inviting as we come alongside our berth, it seems far more desirable than the prospect of further voyaging in the monsoon-whipped waters of the Arabian Sea. We had not expected to be so keen to step ashore!

As later that day we sit in the 'Deccan Queen' express train winding its way up the Western Ghats towards Poona, we find ourselves again and again trying to picture what the coming years will unfold. We little know, but believe that all will be within the plan and purposes of One who is supremely worthy of our trust and utterly dependable. Do we not carry within our hearts the Old Testament promise— "Yet will I be to them as a little sanctuary in the countries where they shall come?" (Ezekiel 11:16) That is enough.

### *A Difficult Start*

Few missionaries would wish to have their first year of overseas service again. No subsequent year can be quite like the first—none quite so long, none experiencing such frequent homesickness. None demanding the almost overwhelming daily adjustments to a land vastly different from one's own. How often we pray simply for what I like to call the grace of elasticity—the ability to bend, to accept, to unlearn; the tolerance to perceive intentions and understand motives, to re-orientate attitudes and thinking. All are necessary in order to adjust to innumerable situations completely foreign to our Western upbringing. Take the domestic side for instance. Our 'quarters' is far better than we had expected, but completely devoid of the conveniences we take for granted in our homeland. There is no refrigerator, no washing machine or dryer, no hot water system, nor any smaller 'essential' domestic appliances. Instead of a tiled-in bath, we use a large galvanized tin tub. There are no built-in closets or cupboards. Instead of an electric oven we use a coke-burning *sigri*. This is a cement 'stove' about a cubic foot in size with a large hole in the top and on one side. In this we will light a charcoal and coke fire. When Eva wants to bake she precariously places her slightly larger tin oven on top of the sigri. Newspapers and an asbestos sheet are placed on top of the oven to help hold the heat in. There is no way of controlling the heat except by fanning the flames in the sigri. Sometimes the baking ends up with soot on it or burned on the bottom and uncooked on the top. Amazingly it often turns out well.

We also have a small kerosene stove on which we boil our water. Finally, there is Anthony, our cook. And what a cook! Anthony, bless his heart, is about 60, and 20 years earlier had worked for the British Army. His most unmilitary appearance disturbs us at first, as he pads around the house with bare feet, stubby beard, unruly hair and shirt tails flapping outside his wide, unpressed trousers.

The preparation of food is an initial nightmare. We discover that all drinking water and milk must be boiled, and uncooked vegetables and fruit is washed in potassium permanganate or salt water for 20 minutes, or peeled. No longer can we drive to a spotless supermarket; now we begin bicycling to a bazaar, with its noise, smells, bartering, congestion and dirt. No longer do we pick up meat lying pre-wrapped within refrigerated shelves. Now it is placed on a wooden slab or tree stump, exposed to heat and flies, and slapped into our bare hands if we forget to take a plastic bag.

Buffalo milk comes unpasteurized, unbottled and watered down, and one has continually to rebuke the milkman. On one occasion the 'dudhwalla' blithely explains the 50 percent water content in the morning's milk by saying, "You see, Memsahib (Madam), it rained last night and the buffalo got wet."

Then there is the continual battle against mosquitoes, lizards, rats, flies, ants and cockroaches. Least disliked are the lizards which are generally ignored because they devour many insects in the course of their daily diet. However, if one falls unseen into the curry as it is being cooked, the results might be fatal to any unfortunate consumer. (We read in the newspaper of a family of eight who died in this way.)

Cockroaches are a constant enemy. Up to two-and-a-half inches in length, these beetle-like pests thrive in hot climates, and although we scrub and 'DDT' our tables and cupboards frequently, it is impossible to eradicate them. Enjoying dinner at the home of some kind national friends one day, I discover one of these voracious insects floating in my soup. In mentioning this to a Swedish neighbour, he jokingly comments that here is a standard by which one can tell how long a missionary has been overseas. If the unfortunate recipient leaves everything he is still in his first five-year term. If he eats the soup and leaves the cockroach, he is a second term missionary. If he is a veteran he eats the lot! On this basis my first-year adjustment rating is quite fair; I eat half the soup, carefully avoiding the cockroach, before giving up.

What stories can be told of adjusting in that first year to monsoon conditions when clothes won't dry and many things become mildewed. Or of the hot season when children are covered in prickly heat and parents in perspiration. What memories of 'dhobies' who wash one's uniform 'whites' by thrashing them against stones, invariably knocking buttons off, and rarely returning them on time. Or of sudden sickness and high fevers and no telephone or transportation, but fortunately a devoted doctor when we reach the mission hospital, three miles away.

Not least of our difficulties is that of an unknown language, compounded by an equally indecipherable script. Inevitably, this limits easy communication and is a daily trial. There are misunderstandings which relentlessly consume nervous energy. Later, of course, some of these misunderstandings provide hilariously funny anecdotes. Take, for example, the experience an overseas territorial commander's wife has with her cook. One day she discovers him straining the soup through one of her husband's socks, and thinks she successfully conveys her displeasure. Imagine her dismay, however, when a few days later the cook is again seen straining soup through her spouse's footwear. When a further desperate attempt is made to forbid the use of socks for straining food, the cook simply smiles and gives an answer which leaves Mrs. T.C. speechless—"No worry, Memsahib, this not Sahib's clean sock."

We are fascinated by the variety of Indian dress and people, but appalled by the sharp contrasts. Beautiful Parsi women in exquisite saris. Frightfully deformed and diseased beggars with scarcely a rag on their backs. Often only a few steps separate palatial, ultra-modern homes from indescribably primitive mud-thatch dwellings. A few imported late model cars share the cluttered roads with hordes of pedestrians, donkeys, buffaloes, bullock carts, horse garis, motor rickshaws, sheep, goats and cows. We see one hundred and one new sights. Women balancing heavy loads on their heads. Children picking up dung in their hands for use, after drying, as a cooking fuel. Unkempt, hungry pavement dwellers. Perspiring coolies, pushing or carrying incredible loads.

Within two weeks of arrival I depart on my first audit trip to Madras (now Chennai), assisting the I.H.Q. Auditor for South

Asia. There are many travelling adjustments. We take our own bedrolls and flasks of drinking water. The trains, pulled by old Canadian or Polish steam engines, are unbearably hot, dirty and crowded. The stations are a bedlam of noise and confusion. Numberless groups of intending passengers squat on the platforms shared with beggars, dogs, goats and sometimes monkeys. Hawkers move up and down with their fruits, toys, and refreshments shouting their individual cries with an ear-splitting abandon that frequently shatters any tenuously-held night time sleep. Evangeline, at home alone with our little daughter, misses the telephone, the radio, television, and me. She hates the eerie night-time sounds of Hindu festival celebrations, pariah dogs fighting, and chanting mourners shuffling to the nearby burning ghat.

But hardest of all to bear in that first unforgettable year is news from home. Less than a month after arrival in India we receive the disturbing news that my mother is not well. A few weeks later she is in hospital for a lengthy and serious operation. Then, five months after our arrival in India, and just prior to an audit trip to Pakistan, a letter comes to the audit office in Poona requesting that I be warned that the end is not far away. It is in kindness that Colonel and Mrs. Leslie Russell decide to withhold the news until after Christmas. But at 2:00 a.m. on the Saturday after our departure, Eva hears the sound of the telegram boy ringing his bicycle bell outside our gate. Mother has been 'promoted to Glory.' After waiting sleeplessly until daybreak, Eva passes the news to Mrs. Russell who immediately wires her husband in Lahore. We are having dinner after the Sunday morning meeting when the telegram is opened and, at a convenient moment, the Colonel takes me out into the garden and shares the sad news.

Dear Mother, her last audible words are, "God bless my boys," and, "Precious Jesus." How we miss her regular weekly letters in the ensuing weeks. How far we feel from home at that time of deep sorrow, when news seems to trickle through so slowly. As letters come by seamail, it is two months before we learn significant details about the service of remembrance and commitment.

But there is more sorrow for us to bear in that first difficult year. Without any forewarning, another telegram arrives eight months later. Father had died suddenly while visiting England. We cannot be sorry for Father, courageously battling loneliness since Mother died; but to us it is a hard blow that only time can heal.

Yes, that first year of missionary service seems unending. Its numerous new experiences and adjustments demand unexpected reserves of adaptability and grace. How often we feel like catching the next ship home. But looking back we can only thank God that lack of funds, personal pride, and the prayers of homeland friends and family make this impossible. And far more than we can say, we are helped and aided by the veteran missionary officers with whom we work, and a host of wonderful missionary associates. Increasingly, too, there are many gracious Indian friends surrounding us whom we love and respect.

### *In Journeys Most Frequent*

Just a few doors down the road from our bungalow is a large, two-storey building. Lovely Swedish mission folk occupy the ground floor, and operate a Christian bookstore in Poona's cantonment area.

A sign near the side entrance to the building indicates that upstairs is the Registered Office for The Salvation Army, India. It is the home of the international auditor and his wife, with one room set aside as an office.

I soon discover the unique position of this Registered Office within the sub-continent. Our relationship to the then four 'territories' of India is something like the relationship the Vatican has to Italy—within, yet distinct from. Though situated in the Western India Territory, the combined audit, editorial and registered office comes directly under the oversight of the International Secretary for South Asia, in London.

Travelling is a normal part of our monthly program. Just ten days after arriving in India I leave home on my first audit trip with Colonel Russell to Madras! Fortunately, Eva is helped by the motherly care of Mrs. Russell, and subsequently by many other wonderful friends. Nevertheless, few missionary mothers would wish to experience such constant separations in the earliest years of overseas service and family life. Both Howard and Graham are born in Poona during this period. I look back with admiration and amazement at Eva's courage and cheerfulness through it all.

Because this appointment lasts seven years, I think some description of these travels, which take us to territorial centres throughout South Asia, needs to be recalled. Come with me, then, on an audit trip to Pakistan in the early 1960s.

The final two or three days in Poona are inevitably hectic as we clear outstanding business, put *The War Cry* 'to bed,' and tie up all the ends prior to departure. A two-day journey north via Bombay and Delhi brings us to Amritsar, where the Sikh community has its renowned Golden Temple.

Breakfast in the station restaurant prepares us for a 20-mile taxi ride on the Grand Trunk Road out to the border checkpoint at Wagha. Here an emigration officer sits under the shade of a tree to check our passports, before we move on for luggage inspection. Coolies (porters) then help us carry our luggage along a lengthy stretch of no-man's land to a point midway between the two check points. A solitary Indian soldier stands alongside his Pakistani counterpart as the coolies dump our belongings on the ground and we pay them. Then Pakistani porters pick up our suitcases and bedding rolls and carry them, balanced on their heads, to their security officials.

It is good to catch sight of the brilliant red T.H.Q. Landrover waiting for us, and it is not too long before we are travelling the last dozen and a half miles of our journey to this distant centre. Near the border we see a sign erected to commemorate the terrible loss of life in this area at the time of Partition in 1947. A mass migration of homeless, bewildered Hindus moving in one direction, clashed with a hysterical, frightened horde of Moslem refugees moving in the other. The result was an indescribable carnage in which tens of thousands of men, women and children lost their lives. It was a tragic end to the British Empire era, and a dark dawning of independence for two great countries.

We receive a warm welcome on entering the fine Salvation Army headquarters compound at Lahore, and quickly settle down to the business of the visit. There is little to say about the somewhat tedious days of audit which follow, except that peculiarities we face in this part of the world include checking many vouchers in a foreign language and script. How do you verify receipts signed by thumb impressions due to illiteracy? (Outside auditors did not check our accounts at this time.)

But if our daytime activities are somewhat monotonous, our kind hosts do their best to make the visit memorable in moments of relaxation. Perhaps we will be taken to see places of historic or general interest such as Lahore Fort, Jehangir's Tomb or Shalimar Gardens. We have opportunity to shop on the broad, attractive Mall, to see the life-giving canals that run like veins on a leaf from the vicinity of this ancient city. We observe old men lying lazily on charpoys, or squatting together sharing a communal 'hookah' pipe. And women observing strict purdah, hidden behind burqas that have only a crocheted eyepiece to see through. At sunrise and sunset we hear the voice of the mullah ringing out his call to prayer with melancholy mystery from atop the nearest mosque. We feel something of the pulse of Pakistan.

An incident occurs during our visit that sharpens our awareness that the pulse of Pakistan is changing. It is a crisp December day and about two dozen of us gather for the Sunday morning open-air meeting. The youthful instrumentalists of the Central Hall band represent about half of our strength, while headquarters officers, corps comrades and we Poona auditors completed the group.

There is nothing unusual about the early part of the meeting; the salvation witness is similar to a thousand others taking place that same Sunday in every part of the world where the Army flag flies. A fine crowd has gathered to listen to the music of the band, the testimonies and the brief message from God's Word.

Then there is a dramatic change. A tall, slightly-built spectator with dark hair, close-trimmed moustache and sharp features suddenly moves away a few paces and begins to harangue the onlookers for listening to 'heretics.' Supported by several accomplices, he soon disturbs our meeting enough to necessitate a rather abrupt termination. However, it is to the strains of, "Joy, joy, joy, there is joy in The Salvation Army," that we march away with undismayed step to attempt another stand.

Down the street and around the corner we commence again. But no sooner do we gather a goodly group of inquisitive hearers than we spy the 'opposition party' furiously cycling toward us. The hostile leader, throwing his cycle to the ground immediately renews the contentious commotion of the previous stand. The excitement heightens when he breaks into our circle and urges the crowd not to listen to 'these Christ-proclaimers,' reminding them of the cardinal Islamic tenet—'There is one God and Mohammed is his prophet.' The intruder and his accomplices cannot be persuaded by quiet reasoning to leave our ring. Several young bandsmen are only too keen to use other means to assist the prompt dispatch of our unpleasant and discourteous antagonists!

With a rather tense atmosphere developing, discretion again dictates an orderly withdrawal. The bandmaster calls out, "Number Four, boys," and we are soon marching briskly along Queen' Road playing a tune called 'Duke Street'!

I suppose I've played Duke Street hundreds of times. I remember, when commissioned a young people's bandsman, contributing with four other boys to an exuberant exposition of how we thought the tune should go. The suffering audience gave us an ovation that evidenced their gratitude and relief that the ordeal was over. Since then, with somewhat improved skill and accuracy perhaps, I have pumped out almost every part on all sorts of instruments in all sorts of bands, as far removed as Kentville and Colombo, Berlin and Bombay.

On no occasion can I recall a comparable thrill to that which gripped me on this memorable Sunday morning in Lahore. There we are, a truly international group of Salvationists—fifteen Pakistanis, four Canadians, three South Africans, two Britishers and one Australian—withdrawing from heckling and harassment, yet sounding out the triumphant words associated with the tune Duke Street—

*Jesus shall reign where'er the sun*
*Doth his successive journeys run;*
*His kingdom stretch from shore to shore,*
*Till sun shall rise and set no more.*

Our encounter that Sunday morning with militant Islamic fundamentalists is probably the beginning of restrictions imposed on our outdoor witness. The police will not agree to give any protection if future incidents occur, and advise that such activities be confined within our own gated compound.

Within a few days our visit draws to an end, and the moment comes when, with bags and bed-rolls packed once again, we commence the long journey home. Travelling is invariably hot, dirty, uncomfortable and tiring by Western standards, but it is made more bearable now that our faces are turned homeward to Poona, and Christmas is just around the corner!

### *Happy to be Home*

It is Sunday. In spite of arriving home halfway through the night, the auditors rise with their families in order to attend the only English meeting of the week. This is held in the Central Corps attached to Poona divisional headquarters, and takes place at 9:30 a.m. in order to avoid the hottest part of the day. We have no band or songsters (choir), but a lovely devotional spirit pervades the little Napier Road hall in which about thirty of us—the majority being missionaries from other societies—are gathered.

Following the meeting, the seven officer-missionaries living in Poona take this weekly opportunity for coffee together. There is always news to share! The hottest hours of the early afternoon provide an opportunity for rest, reading and letter writing before tea. An often absent daddy is then able to take his children for a pleasant walk before he cycles off to a nearby corps for the evening Marathi meeting.

I do not get too much inspiration from the meeting, for I understand little of what is said. Further, the backless benches are uncomfortable, there is no musical accompaniment to the bhajans, and many of the children, who are in the majority, are fidgety. But it is an opportunity to identify with national comrades, and share something of the burden of their difficult ministry.

Monday morning at the office the pace quickens. The initial problem is to settle priorities. As cashier/accountant I clear several important matters before assisting with *The War Cry*, which also demands urgent attention.

Publishing an English language *War Cry* in Asia presents its own peculiar problems. It is inevitable, for instance, that a lot of editing is required before copy received from six different territories is ready for composing. Further careful editing is required when the galleys are returned from the press, as the poor understanding of English that many Indian compositors have, leaves them prone to many mistakes. It is a compositor's error, for instance, which described a former chief of the staff as 'second-in-command of the world-wild Salvation Army!'

One of my tasks is to visit the press, a distance of three-and-a-half miles each way. For almost four years I do this on cycle and, in torrential rain or under burning sun. Stamina is crucial. The eventual purchase of an office Lambretta scooter for the office is a day of high celebration, though the discomforts of monsoon rain and scorching sun continue.

Business calls are also a time-consuming and often a frustrating part of life. Experience has taught me the wisdom of planning half-a-day and half-a-dozen calls every time I venture down town. By so doing, I can hope that the trip will not be entirely fruitless. The scenario might go like this.

I energetically set out full of optimism to complete several business matters. First call is the income tax office. They have promised that our tax clearances for an audit trip to Ceylon will be ready. But, of course, they aren't. I ask some questions—

"Not ready yet? What's the trouble?"

"Assessment not completed. How long have you been here?"

"Five years—it's right on that form."

"Achcha (okay), well, we need a guarantee."

"But the guarantee is right here."

"Oh, I see, the Salvation Army guarantees..."

"Yes, The Salvation Army guarantees us."

"How long are you going—three months?"

"No, two weeks, just two weeks and that is also right on this form."

"Ha. Achcha. And you leave Poona when?"

"Next Friday."

"And when do you get back?"

"Here's the date" (pointing to detail), "April 12."

"Well the Salvation Army guarantees you, does it not?"

"Yes," (for the umteenth time) "The Salvation Army working in 71 countries around the world guarantees us!"

"Achcha. When can you come again?"

"Look, my friend," I conclude, raising my hands in utter defeat, "I've already worn a track from my house to your office, but if you promise the certificate will definitely be ready tomorrow, then I will come."

"Then come tomorrow."

I hurry on to the bank, and present a cheque to be cashed. Perhaps things will be better here. After waiting half-an-hour and reading several 'Digest' articles (I had quickly learned the wisdom of taking reading material with me), I decide some investigation is necessary. The cheque, it appears, is still being queried, and the accountant wants to question me.

"How is it you have these problems?" I ask in dismay.

"But we don't know you and must verify your signature."

"You don't know me?" I expostulate. "Why, I've been paying you a visit every month for almost six years now."

"But we can't find your signature verification card," the accountant politely answers.

"Excuse me," I say, unable to hide an anticipatory smile of triumph, "but if you will look in the back of that file over in the corner, you will find my signature." And sure enough, they do! The gracious apologies that follow almost make it all worthwhile!

Then round to the bank's refund section for an investment refund, but no success. Another signature required—come back tomorrow! Then on to the travel agency for tickets promised. "Sorry, not ready, come back tomorrow." I cycle on to the printers about some stationery already ten days overdue. "Sorry, our machine broke down, can you come back again in two days time?" I bravely smile, and promise.

As I stagger into the house late for lunch, it is wonderful to find a warm welcome and a pleasant reminder that it is my birthday. And surely I can be forgiven for being a little surprised when an unhesitating affirmative reply is received to my question, "Is dinner ready?" I almost expect the answer to be, "Come back tomorrow!"

During these days at home I try to squeeze in a few Hindi lessons, as does Eva. One day I have an enlightening conversation with our pundit. I am translating the sentence, "Mohan and Solan are good because they are Christians." Privately I am thinking that it is rather an unwise sentence for the publishers to include in their textbook; it can infer that only Christians are good—an unfair presumption.

However, as we move to the next question the pundit interrupts me and says, "Excuse me, but can you tell me why that sentence is basically true? In my lifetime I have known many people of many religions intimately. I also know a lot about our Eastern religions. But tell me, why is it that Christians are more honest and truthful and trustworthy than people of other religions? I am a Sindi and follow my faith, but even my own people do not practise their tenets like Christians do."

On the spur of the moment I give him three answers: we are helped by the positive teaching of the Bible, by the peerless example of our Saviour, Jesus Christ, and by the empowering presence of His Spirit in our lives. Our little conversation brings home to me the awareness that there are many in India who not only admire us. They are in fact, or in part, secret Christians themselves. I later discover that the pundit has a picture of Christ hanging in his home.

A similar conversation takes place with our Parsi landlord. One day he says to us, as he admires a picture in our living room of Sallman's Head of Christ, "I live by Christian standards. I do not do anything underhand. I know that one day I shall have to stand before my Maker and give an account of my life. I am not a Christian but I have five Bibles in my house, and seek to live by its teaching."

There are few conversions to Christianity it often seems. But witnessing Christians are unquestionably having a leavening influence upon the religious and secular life of the people of India, that ought to give disciples of Jesus today much affirmation and encouragement.

One of Eva's most satisfying and rewarding weekly activities is to help with, and then be responsible for, a Marathi women's home league. The thirty regular members are desperately poor, and the dilapidated schoolroom where the meetings are held is depressing by Western standards. To the home leaguers, however, this is a highlight event of the week, a refreshing oasis in their desert-like existence.

The women, who know how to smile despite poverty and hardship, appreciate especially the efforts of 'Captainbai' to speak to them in Hindi, and the instruction she gives to a newly-formed group of timbrelists.

Great excitement comes to our home during this first term in India by the birth of Howard in 1961 and Graham in 1963. Both are born at a little Church of Scotland mission hospital in the heart of Poona, managed for many years by a dedicated Scottish woman doctor. In spite of polio and the necessary use of a cane, Dr. Winifred Bailey fulfills her ministry with untiring devotion. We can never forget the love and care this devoted doctor gives to our family when we urgently require medical care.

How calmly and wisely she directs a large group of volunteers who come to her assistance when, without warning, the hospital is flooded to its upper level (18 feet) by a nearby dam burst. Eva has an appointment at the hospital with little Howard that day. Providentially, she forgets! We spend days cleaning up the mud and debris, and washing interior walls.

Of course, the boys add enormous joy to our home and, with their big sister, Heather, are comfortable with their surroundings and lifestyle. Leisure time is spent without television, telephone or automobile. Surprisingly, I doubt whether it is enjoyed any the less. We learn to appreciate the simpler things of life, like verandah conversation with friends, cycle rides with the children, tennis, kite-flying, visiting the zoo, Scrabble, reading and listening to our tape recorder. Visiting an air conditioned ice cream shop is a rare treat.

After a homeland furlough we return with a transistor short wave radio. We quickly become keen radio fans, listening avidly to the B.B.C., Voice of America, and Far Eastern Broadcasting

Company. How we enjoy a short Salvation Army broadcast picked up on the latter station every Sunday lunchtime from Manila! It is only a freak weather condition that allows us on one occasion actually to hear a C.B.C. broadcast beamed to the Arctic.

The days at home fly by and, all too quickly, it is time for me to pack my bags again and be off on what a little girl in our home calls, "another territorial orbit!"

It cannot be said that our first term of service in India passed by 'all too quickly.' Personally, the climate and lifestyle have drained me of energy and my weight has gone down to 122 pounds. We have constantly dreamed about homeland furlough, and excitement and planning increases as that initial five years overseas inches closer to completion.

About a year before returning to Canada it is necessary to make a decision regarding further missionary service. International Headquarters desires us to return. We know there is a desperate shortage of missionary officers in South Asia. We have adjusted to India and love the people. Our hearts know what our answer has to be.

In the meantime there is a wonderful voyage from Bombay to Vancouver via the Far East to anticipate. Our journey will take five weeks, and then there will be five marvellous months with family and friends. We are tired and quite drained of energy as we step on board the P. & O. liner *Chusan* to commence our voyage home. The next few weeks are like a taste of heaven, even though our three children in turn catch the measles, putting us all in isolation. But we thank God for blessings beyond our deserving in the years behind us, and have full confidence of His powerful presence in the years ahead.

## *REFLECTIONS*

After only three years of marriage and five years of service as Salvation Army officers, we little expect the stunning request to serve in India. Our hesitancy and turmoil of heart can well be understood.

If we had said, 'No,' our lives would still have been rich in worthy service. But is it sufficient always to live within our comfort zone?

For a couple of years we wonder if we have made a mistake. But our commitment to stay is secure, and at the end of our first term we happily commit ourselves to further service in India. Our lives have been broadened and enriched immeasurably.

## Chapter 4: 1964 - 1973

## The India Road Continues

### *Off to Hill School*

We are standing on the platform of Poona railway station. The Madras Express has just arrived from Bombay. "I don't want to go alone," says six-and-a-half year-old Heather in the final minutes of family conversation.

"But you won't be alone," reassures her mother, "You know Jackie, and Gillian, and the two little Napper girls."

"Yes, but I wish I could take my two brothers," Heather replies. D-Day minus five minutes could scarcely hold more suppressed tension.

There are moving moments as the train whistle blows and green flags wave. Children hug their parents, and then quickly clamber onto the train. As the Express begins to move slowly out of the station, a cluster of young folk wave frantically from the carriage window, while their parents, whose smiling faces hide aching hearts, respond with equal enthusiasm. Heather is subdued but without tears. No doubt the fact that her daddy is still with her as a group escort makes this initial break a little easier.

It is trite to say that missionary service involves sacrifice. Officers and lay-Salvationists accepting appointments abroad are naturally prepared to leave behind the luxuries of life at home as they move into less-privileged environments. They are well aware that orientation into a foreign culture, taxing climate and unknown situations will involve a degree of hardship, loneliness and frustration.

But there is one sacrifice in some missionary appointments that involves a total commitment difficult for even the most devoted and consecrated heart—the commitment of one's children to boarding school in the hills. In India this takes place at, or soon after, the age of five. To part with one's children at such an early age involves a surrender and sacrifice probably without parallel. One feels something of the deep heartache of Abraham as he prepared to offer Isaac to the Lord. The temptation to ask 'why is this necessary' is difficult to overcome. One is well aware, though, that the beneficial climate and environment in the hills, and the superb British curriculum education at hill school, is in the best future interests of the child.

Fortunately, we are able to complete our first term of overseas service before making our own costly and reluctant surrender. For many months we do our best to prepare heart and mind for the inevitable day when our eldest child, Heather, will join the hill school party travelling from the Poona district after the Christmas holidays. That poignant day has arrived. I will be one of three parent-escorts for the 18 children, whose ages ranged from five to fifteen.

With special care and concern, in our morning devotions, we commit our only daughter to the Lord. Thereafter, for some hours, busy packing activity relieves us from over-obvious tensions. A casual children's conversation at lunch time, however, shakes our superficial equilibrium. Heather is trying to encourage a younger brother to go to his little kindergarten school alone after she has gone. She climaxes her argument—"Anyway, Howard, you should be grateful. At least you can come home from school and eat your food here and sleep here. I can't do that. When Christmas is finished I go to school, and then I don't come back until the next Christmas." And with that, her mummy found an excuse to leave the table.

But now the tension-filled moments of departure have come and gone, and my escort duties commence. It is time to get the bedding rolls out and settle the children down for the night. Imagine my surprise some hours later, when glancing out of the train window at a midnight halt, I see four of the older boys nonchalantly standing on the station platform! I rush out and join them until the train is ready to move off, and then persuade them not to leave the train again unless I know. The boys readily agree and, although somewhat restless, soon settle down for the night.

At daybreak we arrive at Guntakel, and the children, after strapping up their bedrolls, begin tucking into the food their mothers have carefully packed for the journey, and drinking the precious water in their flasks. Eating, together with reading and playing games, fills up most of the hot day for the youngsters, and by late afternoon we reach Arkonam Junction. Here we have a five-hour stop-over prior to boarding the Nilgiri Express. To fill in the time at this dirty and unattractive station, we give the children a supper of egg and chips in the restaurant, and then take them for a long walk.

I also spend some time in the stationmaster's office trying to discover what has happened to our reservations. There are no onward bookings at all for our Poona group. Fortunately, a party from Bombay kindly promises to squeeze our ten smallest children into their accommodation. On time the train noisily enters the station, and after some hectic scurrying, the eight of us remaining find a four-berth compartment that we manage to crowd into for the overnight journey to Mettapalayam, at the foot of the hills.

Inevitably, there is a mad crush and rush at 'Metty,' as school parties from all over India converge here to catch the narrow-gauge Swiss hill train. This will carry them on the last stretch of their long journey back to school. To arrange the transfer of trunks and hand-luggage for 18 young folk, see that the large pieces are properly checked through, and scramble for seats on the hill train requires half-an-hour or so of herculean effort. This is wonderfully and immediately compensated for, however, by an awareness of invigorating, exhilarating mountain air as the little train begins to chug its way almost 7,000 feet up the enchanting Nilgiris. A cogged centre track helps the amazing little engine safely to climb gradients as steep as 1 in 12.50! Though all 18 of us are jammed into a tiny eight-seat compartment, our discomfort is offset by the excitement of beautiful scenery and the proximity of journey's end.

Teachers are waiting at Coonoor station with taxis to help the children on the last lap of their 1,000-plus-mile journey to Hebron School. Heather goes on ahead while I sort out the luggage. By the time I see my six-year old daughter again, she has had a bath, changed into clean clothes, and is unpacking in her new dormitory. She then comes out with me to the front lawn for a final chat. When the supper bell rings a little time later, she gives me a hurried kiss and, without looking back, rushes off with her friends to the dining room. As I pass through the arched gateway and down the road, there is a lump in my throat and a reluctance in my step. I nevertheless thank the Lord for the dedicated, devoted staff who bring a wonderful Christian atmosphere to the care and education of missionary children.

After an overnight stay in Coonoor, I take the afternoon train to Madras where I am to join the Army's international auditor for ten days of business. As the Express speeds through the night I am acutely conscious that each mile is separating me further and further from my daughter. Each minute she is being taken more completely out of the care of her mummy and daddy and into the care of a tender, loving heavenly Father.

Naturally, Heather is in our thoughts constantly in these early days of initial separation, and the letters Eva and I exchange give an insight into the deepest feelings of missionary parents that no other words can better describe.

Heather's mummy begins a letter from Poona: "I wonder how poor little Heather is? I think of her every minute of the day. This place is a morgue without her, and with you away too, I feel almost too wretched to write. I have put Heather's picture in the living room now, and Howard said to me yesterday, 'I don't like that picture Mummy...Heather just sits and looks at us. She doesn't talk or smile or run about. It's just a pretending Heather. I want to see the real Heather again!'"

Immediately I reply, "I too have been thinking much about Heather and the difficulty of adjusting to this initial break." I then try to share some positive, helpful thoughts. Most significantly, "We started out together accepting implicitly and completely Romans 8:28 ('All things work together for good to those who love the Lord...') for every situation of our united lives. I do not believe God will fail us now."

My letter concludes, "If we see Heather in May with rosy cheeks and putting on weight and altogether doing well and settling in happily, this will further help us to see again, God working (not necessarily to our liking) but for good. And we can be sure that many Canadian friends are praying for us continually."

Other matters are also causing some concern. For Eva, "Graham was very ill throughout last night, his little body was burning and his breath came in quick rasps." For me, "You may have heard about the language riots here. Curfew has been imposed in Madras and things are quite bad. However, please do not worry, for we are safe and will be careful."

The best tonic for these depressing, difficult days came in the first letter postmarked 'Coonoor'! The one, long unbroken sentence, printed in pencil says, "Dear Mummy and Daddy I like school we have a new class room we call our new white rabbit Poppy are you happy? my friend is Mary An with lots of love from Heather xoxoxoxoxoxo."

Heather's letters, eagerly anticipated, continue to come regularly each week, soon becoming longer and more interesting. After a month or so we adjust ourselves to her absence, and by that time we are receiving letters like this one:

"Dear Mummy and Daddy, Thank you for your letter Miss Tallett halps me to write the hard words and I am eating ol of mi breakfast up because I like it and I like being in school is grmam better or not I hop he is better now I must tal you sump thing a bawt school on friday it was Melodie Lenrd birthday and we had a nis cack the birthday cack and the bell has gon now sow I must gow so god biy lots of Love from Heather xoxoxoxoxoxo."

Our minds are finally and completely set at rest when, three months later, we travel to Coonoor ourselves to spend furlough days with our daughter at Surrenden, the Army's holiday home and conference centre, a couple of miles from Hebron. It is an unforgettable moment when, having shared a parents' tea at the school immediately on arrival, we walk with eager steps up the sloping path to the playground and suddenly see a blond little schoolgirl leaping into our arms! We are thrilled to discover that she has colour in her cheeks, has put on weight, has settled in wonderfully and is happy. Can we desire more?

Children, ready for Grade 1 education, usually go off to Hebron Hill School at the age of five. The date of school year commencement naturally results in some variance. Howard was five-and-a-half when he left home for hill school, and Graham, two years later and very keen to join his sister and brother, was three weeks short of being five. Eva was an escort for both of them and the heartache hardly lessened. But with increased knowledge of the school's dedicated overseas staff, academic excellence and hugely beneficial environment, we could not doubt its longterm justification.

### Holidays in the Hills

'Buttress Castle' and 'Surrenden' are magical names in the memory of hundreds of missionary officers who have served in the Indian sub-continent. They are names that recall enchanting scenery, spiritual refreshment and bodily renewal. To those who know them, they speak of wonderful days away from the heat and toil of the plains, enjoying an invigorating climate, much-needed relaxation and keenly-anticipated fellowship with many friends.

If we do not hesitate in these chapters of personal reminiscence to describe the hardships and sacrifice of missionary service, then we must not fail to record the rewarding experiences and rich compensations which are also ours.

'Buttress Castle' and 'Surrenden' are the homes of rest that The Salvation Army operates for missionary officers who, of necessity, remain in South Asia for their five annual holiday periods between homeland furloughs. Though both homes are unpretentious and modestly furnished, their surroundings are delightful: the former at Naini Tal in the Kumaon Hills of Northern India, and the latter at Coonoor in South India's Blue Mountain district. From Naini Tal one can view the mighty snow-capped Himalayas, while world-famous tea plantations cover many of Coonoor's less rugged hills.

Some outstanding holiday experiences are still remembered vividly. Buttress Castle is set two hundred feet up one of the steep-sloping hills that closely embrace Naini Tal lake, colourfully scattered with rowboats and sailboats. The myriad lights of houses dotted around the nearby, encircling hills, present a charming fairyland picture at night. The daytime view of encircling mountains further contributes to the majestic setting of this popular holiday resort.

Commencing our first holiday at Naini Tal, I pick up Jim Corbett's book, *Man-eaters of Kumaon*. I wish I hadn't! You see, we are furloughing right in the area where the gruesome episodes recorded by Jim Corbett have their origin. In fact, he has his headquarters right in Naini Tal. And seemingly all the man-eating tigers of which he writes—one has no less than 400 human kills to its 'credit'!—operate within a radius of 50 miles of this lovely little hill station. Further, part of the body of a young victim of one man-eater is actually buried in the small shimmering lake that we admire from the verandah of Buttress Castle and around which we blithely promenade almost daily.

At this point of my reading I am beginning to wonder whether we have chosen the most propitious place for a relaxing holiday, and am questioning why headquarters has not equipped us with suitable firearms. However, as I read on I discover some less chilling facts, and courage and confidence are regained. Apparently, man-eaters have not been known in the district for some time now. In favour of Mister Tiger it must be stated that he only turns to a human diet when incapacitated by wounds or old age, and when speed, teeth or claws are impaired.

However, man-eating or non-man-eating, I still do not desire to meet one of these kings of the Kumaon Hills unless he is behind bars. One day, hiking among the surrounding sub-Himalayan hills, a small group of us eventually pause at a little village cafe for liquid refreshment. Spread out on the wall is the skin of a young leopard. With casual admiration we ask the proprietor where he bought such a fine skin.

"Oh," he replies nonchalantly, "I didn't buy it, I shot it—just about a mile from here!" I am glad we plan to take a bus the rest of the way home. My feet are tired!

Of course, hiking is an inevitable occupation at Naini Tal. You can't go anywhere without climbing or descending a slope. It's even a hike to the shops. However, especially pleasurable is the memory of a hike we make to a famous Christian 'ashram' at Sat Tal, meaning seven lakes.

Early one morning we set out from Buttress Castle. Our bus takes us for an hour along exciting mountain roads with endless twists and turns, hairpin bends, steep gradients, sheer drops and breathtaking scenery. Leaving the bus, we scramble several hundred feet down the mountain slope to a winding path, and hike for another hour until the ashram comes into view. There is something especially impressive about discovering this camp in such a remote and majestic setting.

Like a homeland church Bible camp, the Ashram combines helpful spiritual instruction with healthy recreational activity. It is open to persons of any age, color and creed, and participants are called by their first names, prefixed by 'brother' or 'sister.' Thus the eminent co-founder, director and main lecturer is always referred to as 'Brother Stanley.'

We arrived just in time for the morning teaching and discussion periods, held in an octagonal wood-frame building shaped like an outsize Bell tent. About 60 participants sit cross-legged on mats on the floor as does Brother Stanley who faces us, wearing an Indian dhoti. We Salvationist visitors are individually introduced and warmly welcomed.

To sit quietly under the refreshing and instructive ministry of Brother Stanley is a memorable experience. He combines humility with humour, simplicity with spirituality, and an orthodox faith with an original mind. He is constantly making such pithy, pertinent remarks as, "When a man has ulcers, don't ask him what he's eating, but what's eating him;" "It is the un-Christian things that always upset us; it is the Christian things that set us up;" "Hell is portable."

After two stimulating hours we adjourn for lunch, and here again Brother Stanley's conviction that the missionary's function is to Christianize and not Westernize is evident. We take off our shoes before entering and then sit on the floor in front of several low tables raised not more than nine inches from the ground. The fare, naturally, is curry and rice and all the trimmings. Coupled with food for the body, food for the mind intrigues us. Around the walls many plaques bear thought-provoking inscriptions such as—"It is not my responsibility that is important, but my response to His ability;" and "There is enough of everything in the world for man's need, but there is not enough of everything in the world for man's greed."

A quiet period follows lunch, after which we enjoy a pleasant swim in the lake amidst the natural beauty of the densely-wooded hills that surround us. Imagine our surprise when Brother Stanley—although well over 70—happily joins us in the water!

We return to the main house for tea and then regretfully say goodbye to our Ashram friends and shake hands once again with Brother Stanley. Then begins a 90-minute trek to the little mountain village of Bhim Tal where the last bus to Naini Tal is awaiting us.

But who, you ask, is Brother Stanley? Well, he is the distinguished missionary-statesman, Dr. E. Stanley Jones, who spent half a century in India and became a personal friend of Mahatma Gandhi and other outstanding leaders of this great land. He was still spending part of each year visiting the ashrams that have spread to many parts of the world since originating at Sat Tal more than 30 years earlier. Furthermore, he has written more than a dozen widely-read books, perhaps the most notable being *The Christ of the Indian Road*—one that influenced me greatly in earlier years.

Some years later we are privileged to attend a memorial service for this great Christian in New Delhi. Two weeks before his death Dr. Jones had been asked his reaction to a severe stroke he had experienced. "When doctors told William Booth he was going blind," he replied, "the Salvation Army's founder declared that he would serve God with the same zeal and energy as when he had his eyesight—and so will I!"

Holidays in South India also conjure up a host of recollections. Instead of ashrams there are the Nilgiri Conventions which last a week in each of the neighbouring hill resorts of Ootacamund, Coonoor and Kotagiri, and feature well-known evangelists in twice-daily expositional and devotional messages. Hikes are part of our program too, though the objects are not mountain peaks like Snow View and Cheena Peak, but scenic sights such as Khetti Falls, Lambs Rock and the Dhrug.

'Surrenden' is set in more spacious, open ground than its northern counterpart, and has beautifully-kept lawns and flower beds, and tennis and badminton courts. From the annex there is a superb view of Wellington golf course some 300 feet below, and beyond this, undulating hills in every shade of green, from the frosty green of tall eucalyptus to the deep green of waist-high tea bushes.

I doubt whether any Salvation Army holiday home has quite the atmosphere of Surrenden in May. This is the only month of the year from the beginning of February to the end of November when hill school children are re-united with their parents, and families are complete. What excitement there is when, following the school concerts that close the term, taxis roll up at Surrenden and out jump laughing children and happy mums and dads.

The joyful weeks that follow culminate in 'family night,' a riotous evening of fun and frolic and non-stop laughter. For a week preceding the event, anticipation increases in momentum, and lines of doggerel on the breakfast trays stir ill-prepared participants into a fever of activity:

> *'Tomorrow's the day and eight's the hour*
> *When in the lounge starts a fantastic shower*
> *Of items funny, hilarious, bizarre,*
> *Whose fame will spread so very far*
> *That the "History of S.A. volume umpteen"*
> *Will say this night's the greatest that's been.'*

'Hamburgers' (so called) and coffee bring to a grand finale this long-talked-about night of merriment.

A different kind of night, equally enjoyed and remembered, is Sunday evening, when we share a family meeting together. We have come from the far corners of the sub-continent, longing for the renewed contact and companionship of the holiday season. Yet I suggest that no fellowship we share together during this period is as rich in blessing as these treasured gatherings. There is an affinity of spirit and mutual desire for renewed grace and strength that make these moments hallowed indeed. Our own burdens become lighter as we hear of the heart-breaking experiences others have been called to pass through, and yet withal the deep awareness, to which they testify, of God's abiding and unfailing presence.

All too quickly a day comes when bulging taxis return the children to school—the girls to nearby Hebron, the older boys to Lushington, a dozen miles away at Ootacamund. Around the supper table that evening, conversation for the first time is subdued, though we all do our best to hide our feelings. We are glad that for the remaining hours of the day, as well as the following morning we are kept busy packing for our own return.

Soon after lunch more taxis whisk us to Coonoor station, and within three hours we are back on the plains of India at 'Metty.' For some a journey of but a few hours is in front of them, for others the trip home will yet take several days. Uppermost in the thoughts of all of us throughout the journey—and for many days to come—will be a deep gratitude for the provision made by Army leaders, through such holiday homes, for the well-being of overseas officers.

### *Bombay Beckons*

After seven years in Poona, and something like 120,000 miles of audit travelling, it comes as no surprise to receive "marching orders." We are being posted to Bombay (now Mumbai), the "Gateway to India," to oversee the Salvation Army's youth work in Western India.

From a personal point of view Poona (now Pune) is a more desirable place to live than Bombay, being a thousand-plus feet up the Western Ghats and therefore less humid than Maharashtra's capital city. Further, we had lived in the cantonment area that still maintained a well-groomed, British-style military presence, and rural gentleness. Most shops were closed during the early afternoon hours; the hottest part of the day was siesta-time for all sensible citizens. Unfortunately this did not include mad-dogs, Englishmen, and Salvation Army auditors! Pith helmets were also common and sensible head-dress.

Bombay, in contrast, is a city of constant noise and bustle, and Byculla—the area in which we live—is not the most salubrious district of this great commercial city. In fact, Sankli Street, which houses headquarters and most of its staff, is constantly congested with the traffic of life. Its sidewalks, which we walk daily between home and office, is largely occupied by pavement-dwellers.

On the day we arrived, a friend coming to welcome us found a dying man on the pavement outside. She rushed up the stairs to our home and breathlessly asked for any cloths we might have to cover him so that he might die with a little dignity. The welcome greeting was postponed.

Our living quarters, part of a long-standing Salvation Army complex, has six-foot high partitions to separate rooms. Our children can peek over their bunk beds to see if Mum and Dad are awake. The house is devoid of most Western conveniences. We have water for one hour a day, from 5.00 a.m. to 6.00 a.m. It has to be stored, and used sparingly. We quickly learn to use just a few inches of water in a tub to bath, then save that water for washing the clothes, that water for washing the floor, and that water for flushing the toilet! We share the rats, cockroaches and other indestructible vermin common to the neighbourhood.

But we are immensely happy. Instead of being in the comparatively isolated role of our Poona appointment, we are now deeply and directly involved in the work of the Western India Territory. Instead of visiting territorial centres throughout the sub-continent, I am now visiting corps and institutions throughout Maharashtra and Gujarat States.

Eva shares my work to a far greater extent in Bombay and we love planning and undertaking new ventures in the interests of the youth of the territory who come under our care. On the business side we become involved in updating Sunday school and corps cadet teaching materials and resolving government problems relating to the financing of our 60-plus schools. Duties also include preparing officer-candidates for training college, participating in headquarters' boards and councils, and much more.

But it is in meeting young people at the grass-roots level that we find greatest joy. For instance, in Bombay we encourage the young people to research every detail of the initial arrival of Commissioner Frederick Booth-Tucker and his pioneer party at Ballard Pier in 1882. One young man, James Hardman (later becoming an officer after emigrating to Canada) uses his draughtsman skills to prepare an authentic route map of the roads travelled, and initial events in which the pioneer four were involved. Then, on the 86th anniversary, we all walk that route of many miles, pausing periodically to recall the significance of particular places. Even the original headquarters building has been found, and arrangements made for a Salvation Army flag to be flown there, while adult Salvationists join us for a rousing outdoor meeting.

The first all-India Youth Camp held at Hyderabad, Andhra Pradesh, is also a highlight event of those days. Never before have Salvationist young people from every corner of India joined together for several days of unparalleled inspiration, fellowship and bonding. A school compound is used, and facilities are somewhat limited. Try sleeping on the concrete top of a science lab table! I still recall the discomfort.

Then on an out-of-town picnic day, five of us are due to visit the state governor. Frantic efforts to get the bus driver to drop us off at a convenient transfer point somehow fail. In desperation we finally insist on leaving the bus. At the appointed hour, however, we are still walking along a rural road, seeking a phone to contact Raj Bhavan, the state governor's residence. In spite of being three hours late, the governor graciously receives us.

Then there is The Army's international Youth Year and later Children's Year, both of which allow for unusual projects that catch the imagination and enthusiastic support of young people throughout the territory. Artifacts remain of these exciting events.

In Youth Year, groups of youthful cyclists journey from one corps to the next with a logbook, charter and emblems. General Frederick Coutts, who is in Bombay at the beginning and end of the year, signs the Log Book twice in celebratory meetings!

The Children's Charter Chariot Tour is the special attraction of Children's Year in the Gujarat. In a gaily decorated jeep, Eva and I visit 26 corps and conduct 34 meetings in 11 days. An exciting part of each meeting is joining the scrolls. The artistically decorated scrolls bear the signatures of everyone who pledges to support the objectives of this special year. At the end of 1000 miles of mainly village road journeying, the scrolls (one for children, one for adults) total 250 feet in length and carry 2,000 signatures.

Memoirs have to be selective, but on a personal level, two experiences of our all-too-short days in Bombay remain vivid and deserve recounting. Both involve train journeys, one taken by me and one by Eva.

I knew it was going to be a bad journey back to Bombay. The Salvation Army compound at Anand, Gujarat, already has six inches of rain water in places as I leave it and slosh my way to the station. It is a monsoon night, dark and miserable. The only bright thought is that my up-country tour is behind me, and soon the train will be taking me on the overnight journey home.

The crowded third-class carriage is noisy with chatter as I find the sardine-size space allocated to me for sleep. I open my bedroll, and stretch out on the middle section of a three-tier wooden bunk. Dozing off to sleep I become aware, from the now subdued conversation around me, that all is not well. Several fast-flowing rivers lie between us and our destination, and there is some doubt whether the bridges we must cross will be passable.

I wake early in the morning to realize we have stopped, and soon learn that a bridge ahead has collapsed. We can go no further. The train stands on an embankment, isolated and alone amid an inundated countryside. Torrential rain, gale force winds and a vast water wilderness surround us. Houses are collapsing under the pressure of swirling floodwaters. In the distance we can see villagers and their animals struggling to reach higher ground. We can do nothing to help.

After many hours, our train is able to back up some miles to the comparative safety of a little town called Navsari. Most of the town is unreachable from the railway station. Telephone and telegraph communications are completely knocked out. In the station itself there is no food, not even a cup of tea. I am the only non-Indian on the train. Howling winds and bone-chilling rain continue unabated In our carriage, we are all wet, cold and, yes, somewhat anxious. Eva and my headquarters associates in Bombay are also anxious as, unsuccessfully, they seek information about my whereabouts.

For me, there comes a moment when my train companions show a brotherly love and concern that I can never forget. We are all hungry. Out from their cheap suitcases and paper bags they take the special delicacies prepared for loved ones in Bombay. To my amazement, before they eat any themselves, or even give any to their children, they offer me—a stranger—the little they had: sweatmeats, halwa, bhajias, samosas, chivda.

On the third day and after many hungry hours—the shared snacks had long since run out—special buses reach us and take us by a circuitous route to Bombay. I am cold, wet, hungry and exhausted. But what a happy welcome home I receive!

Sometimes I hear armchair critics talk about 'lazy Asians who should practise more birth control and less black marketing.' When I know this is said without any attempt at cultural awareness or deep understanding, my mind goes back to Navsari. For in that raging flood-water incident, as in other hazardous experiences, gracious "Good Samaritan" assistance that I little deserve or expect is given to me by some of India's poorest people.

Eva's most frightening train journey has nothing to do with an unexpected external situation, such as floods or riots. Rather it is personal and life-threatening. She has been journeying for almost 40 hours. It is just before dawn and the Blue Mountain Express from Madras, with many hill school children on board, has another three hours to go before reaching Mettapalayam. Three further hours on the narrow gauge hill train will finally bring them to journey's end at Coonoor.

Eva and two other parent escorts are responsible for the Bombay party. Before leaving Bombay Eva is introduced to a British doctor who is taking his two sons back to school on the same train. On arrival at Madras the doctor finds that his reservations have been given to someone else. Eva and her escort associates are happy to squeeze three more school-bound passengers into their carriage. This was providential.

Now, to have a miscarriage at any time must be frightening enough. But to be hurtling through the night on an Indian train miles from anywhere, and five months pregnant, must surely be an experience that can only be left to the imagination. Eva, travelling with her doctor's permission, knows something is wrong soon after all the children are sleep. She tries in vain to awaken another escort during the night, but the train makes so much noise it is impossible to do so.

It is at an early morning hour when the train halts at a station called Erode. Eva, knowing the crisis point is arriving, manages quickly to awaken a parent friend who fortunately locates the British doctor (Dr. Banks) a few compartments away. The desperate moments which follow need not be described in detail, but God's protective care is evident. The situation is serious. Eva's life is in danger and she must be taken off the train immediately.

Coolies are called to bring a chair and carry Eva to a waiting room. The children are not wakened, but other parents undertake to look after the doctor's sons, our Heather and Howard, and all the other children for whose care Eva has some responsibility.

After some frantic enquiries Dr. Banks discovers that there is an Anglican mission hospital in town. A dilapidated fire engine responds to the emergency call for assistance. A worrying half hour of high drama follows before Eva is in the hospital emergency room and in the care of a British surgeon.

The telegram I receive in Bombay is quite disturbing. Immediate arrangements are made for my travel and the care of our four-year-old son, Graham. Two anxious days later, I am tremendously relieved to see Eva making a steady recovery. Several further days elapse before I leave the hospital and travel to Coonoor to assure our eight-year-old daughter and six-year-old son that all is well. On my return to Erode, Eva is well enough to manage the long journey back to Bombay.

Such experiences of God's loving presence and provision leave an indelible imprint upon one's life, and a strengthened confidence to trust Him in the ever-changing future. And certainly, for Eva and me there is much change to anticipate. In fact, it is just before Christmas that our territorial commander gives us barely a week to pack before taking pro-tem. charge—later to be confirmed—of the training college in Anand, Gujarat.

### *Town of Joy*

Anand is a busy little town, a railway junction, and a centre of thriving Salvation Army activity. There is the famous Emery Hospital and nursing school, divisional headquarters, Booth-Tucker Hall, boarding schools and training college. Down the road the renowned Amul Dairy kindly opens its guest house to our international visitors.

In several Indian languages 'anand' means joy. Dominique Lapierre's epic saga *City of Joy* tells the story of Anand Nagar, one of the poorest and most over-populated areas of the city of Calcutta. At the heart of this seemingly inhuman place, Lapierre finds "more heroism, more love, more sharing, and ultimately, more happiness than in many a city of the affluent West." His book is a remarkable tribute to the thousands of men, women and children who rise above harsh destinies to conquer life with a smile.

What can be said of the vast slum areas of Calcutta (now Kolkata) in particular, can be said of the great sub-continent of India generally. The courage and buoyant optimism of people who live without the many gadgets, conveniences and facilities that we Westerners deem essential to decent living is a constant reminder that 'things' of themselves do not ensure happiness.

Anand, Gujarat is, in fact, more prosperous than many towns in India—though by Western standards most of its people live frugally. But for Eva and me the five years in that community are among the most joyous memories we have. Often it is the simple pleasures of life that bring special happiness. Our youngest son, Graham, for instance, seems to spend every spare moment of his Christmas holidays flying paper kites—they are just about all he has and all he needs!

At the training college our new family includes 55 cadets and more than a dozen babies and children. The cadets are divided almost equally between Marathis and Gujaratis, and double translation is quite a headache. Single and married cadets are also equally divided. Married women with new babies are allowed to discreetly feed them in class. The freedom of single women cadets is necessarily restricted. To satisfy the anxiety of parents who find it culturally difficult to allow their unmarried daughters away from home, the single women are locked in an inner compound overnight.

The old college is a relic of pioneering days. The office was once a horse stable, and our living room a former bullock cart passageway. On the front side of the quadrangular building is the office and living quarters for ourselves and our training officers. Running parallel at the far end of the compound is the lecture room and two classroooms. On the other two sides of the fort-style college premises is cadets' accommodation. Each couple occupies one of the single little connected rooms that are devoid of all furniture except for a rope-laced 'charpoy' bed and small wooden cupboard.

Life is full of happy activity—and surprises! Like the day the cadets are absorbing some heavy theology in the lecture hall when the cry, "Sap, sap" (snake, snake) is heard. Our two employee-cooks are pulling some wood from the open shed alongside the kitchen, before preparing the cadets' noontime vegetable curry and rice. It is Eva who first sees the snake and sounds the alarm. The two women jump away from the woodshed in fright and the six-foot snake quickly slithers under the woodpile again.

All theology is instantly forgotten as the cadets rush out of the classroom, and men cadets with bamboo poles head for the woodpile. Gingerly the wood is removed piece by piece until the moment of supreme excitement. The snake, with hood extended, seeks to escape. A merry and somewhat dangerous pursuit follows. Finally, some triumphant cadets put the dead snake on a fire to be burned, and return reluctantly to their theological cogitations. Eva meanwhile has hurried over to our quarters and grabbed the camera. We have a couple of good pictures of the six-foot long cobra.

The "Undaunted Session" is the name of that first group of cadets we train. It is a name they have to live up to even before college days come to an end.

Excitement is running high as we approach the last week of the session. Then a new undesirable element creeps into the compound—anxiety! Word reaches us of serious religious riots between Hindus and Muslims breaking out in the great Gandhian city of Ahmedabad, just 50 miles north of us. Further news soon comes that Baroda, 20 miles south, is also in the grip of communal disturbances. Sadly and soon, our own town becomes embroiled in the mounting violence that spreads out of control through much of Gujarat State. For several days we live in a stomach-churning atmosphere of fear and tension.

It is with considerable relief as we lie awake one night in the middle of the week that we hear the heavy rumble of military trucks. Troops pour into the town to restore order. It adds to our satisfaction to know that their base is a police station just up the road, and many are quartered in our Salvation Army Emery Hospital compound opposite.

Initially, the curfew is severe and round the clock. This gives us many worries. The Muslim meatwallah (seller of meat) has not dared to come for several days, and vegetables are scarce. Now our wheat flour—used in making chappatties, a staple food—runs low. Thursday evening the cadets sit down to a very unappetizing meal, instead of the long-anticipated grand farewell dinner.

Friday evening there is only enough wheat flour for one more meal. We pray that the Lord will meet our needs in His own way and time. We can do little else. To our great relief the curfew lifts for two hours on Saturday morning—time enough to obtain two precious bags of wheat, have the women cadets clean it, and take it to the grinding shop.

It is necessary for me to return after curfew is reimposed, and I back the jeep as close to the door of the shop as possible. It is the work of a moment for the shopkeeper to partially open his door, help me throw the heavy sacks in the jeep and disappear inside again without being observed by military patrols. What a relief to know that 46 cadets and 12 children will not go hungry after all. Our extremity is God's opportunity.

The whole commissioning weekend is one of unbelievable disruption countered by dauntless optimism. We cannot hold events in our roadside Booth Tucker hall, so we reschedule them to secluded areas of our large Salvation Army compound during non-curfew hours. Even then no relatives can be present. Smart new uniforms are inaccessible at the tailor's shop and everyday uniforms—for some cadets—are behind the doors of tightly closed dry cleaners.

In spite of encountering a series of emergency situations—and even the departure of cadets to their first appointments is a tricky affair—the commissioning ends up as a first class event exceeding our highest hopes and expectations. The sessions' singing of "Christ has need of dauntless soldiers," just before the weekend concludes, is poignantly timely and always to be remembered.

### *Anand Central Corps*

In addition to our training college commitments, Eva and I have responsibility for Anand Central Corps. A most happy and enriching experience.

The corps, one of the strongest in Gujarat, is proud of its Booth-Tucker Hall and its long and colourful history. Within the corps are many fine, well-educated Salvationists who, we feel, should participate more actively in the life of the corps.

For the first time anywhere in India, we believe, a corps council is set up, and no corps officers have a more creative and enthusiastic group than we have. Through a host of novel ideas (like the sale of full-colour Salvation Army calendars) and personal pledging (in a special public meeting) corps members raise thousands of rupees toward renovating and modernizing the Booth-Tucker Hall.

The Council also brings in a system of tithing to improve corps financing. Any doubts about money being recorded honestly is overcome in a culturally acceptable way by showing individual contributions on wall charts. These are updated weekly.

More than this, the council shares in bringing spiritual renewal and revival to the corps. We will never forget the outpouring of God's Spirit upon us after a whole night of prayer. Several days of remarkable Mercy Seat scenes follow, with dozens of people confessing sins and many experiencing an outpouring of joy and empowerment. Meetings continue day and night, and our training college schedule is temporarily set aside.

The then Chief of the Staff, Commissioner Arnold Brown, is a distinguished visitor during our period in Anand. Like many of his predecessors, he had a little 'tummy trouble' while with us (though, let me hasten to add, it did not originate with us!). Eva is able to provide some quick-acting medicinal assistance. We certainly learn to be all things to all people.

When taking over Anand Central Corps I am also given the baton, and the band of about 15 members becomes another rewarding part of my ministry. I recall a happy moment when the band gathers on Anand Railway Station to bid farewell to the visiting Chief. We play one of Commissioner (later General) Arnold Brown's melodies—perhaps with more enthusiasm than tunefulness—when the 'great one' from London arrives on the station platform. The Chief of that day immediately steps into the ring and takes the baton from me, to the great delight of all gathered. How humbling to note that the band sounds better!

Many other incidents linger in my memory of five good years in the Gujarat. Incidents which do not merit detailing in this record, but which nevertheless for Eva and me—and in some cases our children—remain a vivid part of those days. Can we forget the monkeys that constantly bound on the roofs of our college buildings and, initially into our home? Or other uninvited guests— a dead pigeon in the bathroom sink, a snake skin in the dining room, and a live rat in our bed (occupied that night by an important visitor!)

But there are more significant memories, of course. The unbearable heat as we conduct youth councils at Muktipur Colony. The village meetings under starry skies and kerosene lamps. The sea of mud that surrounds us when visiting the primitive, colourfully dressed Bhil people of Panch Mahals district in monsoon time. The rare visits with our children to an air-conditioned ice-cream shop in Baroda.

And on, and on. But here we must stop, and move forward in memory to new challenges that await us in Canada. It is time to give our teenage children an opportunity to settle comfortably into a homeland environment. It would be more difficult for them than we imagined.

## *REFLECTIONS*

Sending off our children to hill school is the most difficult part of our next two terms overseas. It must be said, however, that the decision had already been made before our first term concluded. The implementation nevertheless requires a continuing conviction of 'rightness'.

But what is our reflective thinking now? In some spiritual exercises developed by St. Ignatius of Loyola on the theme of decision-making, he makes the final comment:

"There are times when I have to work out logically the best choice, looking at all the pros and cons. But even when I finish making a choice this way, I should 'feel' comfortable and consoled with the final decision." We felt 'consoled'.

Another decision had to be made near the end of our second term. Should we return again? The Western India Territory expressed a strong desire that we return. We were thoroughly enjoying our ministry, but delayed any confirmation of a return until homeland furlough.

While at Powell River, British Columbia (Eva's home), one of our sons expressed to a friend of ours some unhappiness about returning to India. Desiring some guidance we asked a local doctor to privately discuss the subject with him. To our amazement we later discovered that the doctor had been a student at the same boarding school as our boys. We knew his parents and had been present at his mother's funeral just two weeks before our furlough. What a helpful and providential happenstance! The good doctor recommended to us a shorter term, and this met with the approval of our leaders.

Two changes of appointment occurred during our second term, and both proved immensely rewarding. An original intention was for us to transfer to Calcutta where I was to be financial secretary. I knew innately that I am not a natural finance person, and before the appointment was made had an opportunity to express my uneasiness to the international secretary. He kept this in mind and, without further consultation, we soon found ourselves posted to Bombay to oversee the territory's youth work. I have never regretted making my feelings known in this matter.

## Chapter 5: 1973 - 1982

## Publishing – For Goodness Sake

### *A Last Sea Voyage*

After fourteen-and-a-half years in India there are naturally mixed feelings for us as *MV Victoria* slips away from Ballard Pier, Bombay, and sets a south-westerly course across the Arabian Sea and Indian Ocean. The date is September 8, 1973.

It is not easy to leave behind a part of the world where we have lived about a third of our lives, where Howard and Graham were born, and where we have gained far more than we have given. We are better people for those years, mostly spent as young captains with boundless energy and enthusiasm. Auditing, editing, youth work and training college appointments have all provided the kind of experience that can only lead to personal growth, widened horizons, and potential for effective future service.

After calls at Mombasa and Durban where we enjoy the kind hospitality of Army friends, we see the famous Table Mountain before docking at Cape Town. Here we disembark and are graciously cared for at the Army's newly-opened holiday home at Fish Hoek while awaiting the departure of *SA Oranje* on one of its last voyages to Southampton. This is one of several voyages considerably lengthened due to the closure of the Suez Canal.

There are just a few days to meet some relatives and friends in England before boarding *SS France* on its last passenger voyage to New York. It is the end of an era as shipping lines relunctantly give way to the age of flight. Personally, we always enjoy voyaging and are rarely seasick. After long terms of service with frugal living, and deprived of so much we take for granted in our homeland, the weeks at sea rejuvenate worn bodies and tired spirits.

So our last sea voyage is on the largest liner of that day. *S.S. France* is more than 66,000 tons and quite a contrast to smaller ships we have travelled on between Vancouver (Eva's home is in British Columbia, of course) and India. Once we journeyed via the Far East, once via Australasia, and several times from Montreal via the Atlantic, Mediterranean and Suez Canal. Just once we flew via Athens and Tel Aviv, giving opportunity to spend a few cherished days in biblical surroundings.

It occurs to me, as the Statue of Liberty is seen, that the last time I had passed this famous landmark was as a single young man en route to Canada from England 24 years earlier. I had decided to settle in Canada, land of my birth, and crossed the Atlantic on the *Queen Mary*, another great ship of mid-century years. My mind recalled the undreamed of ways God over-ruled in the affairs of my life in the intervening years including our life-changing India road experience.

### The Joy of Writing

For me there is special pleasure in the Oakville editorial appointment. Something of a family tradition is being repeated. I had been born in Toronto during the 11-year period of my father's posting to the Canadian editorial department from International Headquarters, London, England. Father, Bramwell Coles, was also an increasingly popular Salvation Army composer. Was it in the office between reading proofs and writing reports that, surreptitiously, he jotted down ideas for "Under Two Flags" or some of the many marches and selections for Army bands that became so famous?

Then, too, my eldest brother, Gordon, spent most of his officership career in editorial work. He began in Chicago, then moved to Toronto, before a final transfer to the Editorial and Literary Department in London, England.

My writing efforts began when, as a very young boy in England, I wrote an essay, "Why I would like to be at the coronation" (of King George VI and Queen Elizabeth I). A national newspaper of that day, *The Daily Sketch*, sponsored the competition and I won a consolation prize. My interest in writing developed as the years moved on, aided by father's encouragement and by editorial department mentors such as Lieut.-Colonels Herbert Wood and Eric Coward to whom I will always be indebted.

### *Temporary Criminal Court Assignment*

Many of my articles and reports had already been written for Salvation Army publications before my appointment to the Canadian editorial office. The last two describe my experience as a court worker in Vancouver during the eight-month period between returning from India and the Oakville assignment. They summarize that short but significant Vancouver interlude.

### *Criminal Court Diary*

My first day in a criminal court, remains a vivid, unforgettable experience.

It began at 7:30 one winter morning in our narrow office corridor, where I joined three other court workers in an earnest prayer for God's blessing and guidance. A brisk walk through rainy, pre-dawn darkness brought us to Vancouver's large public safety building. In a matter of minutes we had taken off our coats, picked up the day's court lists, and ascended to upper floor cell blocks.

We entered an interview room and set ourselves up at a large counter placed across one corner. A duty lawyer sat at a small desk in the opposite corner. The otherwise bare room soon filled as two dozen men were brought in—all chain smoking, some cursing and shouting, others listless and anxious. My associates began the arduous task of interviewing them; completing legal aid applications for most, answering questions for many and giving counsel to a few.

What a terrible feeling of claustrophobia came upon me that first day—locked in with men charged with breaking and entering, theft, indecent assault, trafficking in heroin to mention but a few. The desire to scream, 'let me out of here' was almost overpowering. It was a shattering contrast to previous surroundings. But I had to wait and watch for 90 minutes before we were ready to leave and a guard unlocked the door.

With welcome relief but a pounding head, I followed my more relaxed companions down to No.2 Court. Our well-known women's court worker, who had been interviewing in a separate area, joined us. In an ante-room we quickly checked court lists against our legal aid files to ensure that counsel would be present for all remand cases. Moving into the lobby, we gave advice to a number of non-custody people about pleas, adjournments, bail and counsel.

Hurriedly entering No.2 Court by a side door, we bow to the judge before sitting down at a special counsel table in front of the crowded public benches. "Order in Court" has already been called. The morning's long docket of 150 cases has begun. An air of suspense pervades the room as the Crown Prosecutor calls the first prisoner to the dock. The Crown Prosecutor is a key figure in the swift-moving drama that unfolds before the court in the next four hours. Essential and skilled assistance is given by the duty counsel, court clerk, police officers, stenographer, and other official and voluntary court workers. Dominating the whole panorama from his raised dais, is the presiding judge who must constantly consider protection of the public, necessary deterrence and rehabilitation of the offender as he sets bail or passes sentence.

To no small degree, the helpful presence of The Salvation Army's representatives not only assists the smooth running of this busy court, but meets the need for 'grace' which law often cannot provide. Again and again, the judge will seek the aid of, or appreciate information given by, the blue uniformed Salvationists. The lawyers, hurrying in to set trial dates or to present guilty pleas on behalf of their clients, will pause for a whispered conversation with the knowledgeable Salvationist. Their aid will also be sought by a host of other court workers because of their special position, shared with duty counsel, of having interviewed every prisoner before the court appearance.

In the (then called) Salvation Army Correctional Services Department, there are co-workers (officers and lay people) who regularly visit each of the provincial and federal institutions in the area thus providing an important link with the prisoner from first appearance in court to the final day of jail release. The Salvationist court worker has behind him the varied services of the Army across Canada so that at the request of a judge, or by personal representation, an offender can be committed to the care of the city's Catherine Booth Home for Women, or to the Miracle Valley for alcoholics, or to the House of Concord, or to one of a score of similar centres in which the Salvation Army provides Christian based rehabilitation programs.

It is one-thirty before No.2 Court completes its morning role (shared with No.3 Court) as a 'clearing house' for the other nine city courts where most of the law-breakers will eventually face trial. But our work is not yet done. Again we must return to the fifth floor cells to complete some additional work resulting from the morning court appearances. A prisoner who changed his plea now desires legal aid assistance. Another, who will be released on cash bail, has no one to bring the money to the court building for him. A third, detained in custody, is worried about his personal effects left in a rooming-house. Another half hour has gone before the interviews are finished, and we can leave the building.

Somewhat wearily, my companions and I return through still rain-swept lanes to the office for late lunch. I still have my headache. More disturbing, my mind is weighed down by all I have seen on this first day in a criminal court. Again and again I visualize the sad procession of rapists, drug addicts, transvestites, dangerous drivers, shop-lifters, hardened criminals and frightened first time offenders. Can I go back tomorrow? And the next day?

I can, and I must! For where else is there a greater need for compassion and love, for a redemptive ministry which tells the joyous gospel truth that it is never too late to start again.

And I remember the words of Jesus, to whom my co-workers and I have dedicated our lives. 'Inasmuch as you have done it unto one of the least of these my brethren you have done it unto me.' It is enough!

### *Witnessing Without Words*

"Ever since I first saw you Salvation Army folk working in the courts, I have been greatly impressed by what you are doing, and the way you go about it. And I have never ceased to wonder at what makes it all possible."

With these words Tom began to tell me a heart-warming story, as we shared coffee-break conversation in the Public Safety Building canteen. Tom, an immigration official dealing with non-Canadians appearing before the criminal courts of this west coast city, paused and took a sip of coffee before continuing:

"In fact, I spoke to my bishop the other day and asked him this question: 'How can these Salvationists who work in the courts maintain a faith in such a soul-destroying atmosphere? How can they show unfailing compassion to those who show little appreciation, and most often reject their spiritual message? How can they keep such a freshness of attitude and a glow on their features amid this depressing environment? I have watched them carefully, day after day, year in, year out, and they never seem to give up, never seem to lose hope, never appear to change.

"The bishop thought for a long moment before answering my question. Then he said, 'I will tell you this, Tom; these people truly believe that Christ Jesus came into the world to save sinners. To them it is more than a biblical statement, it is a truth to which they must witness. And while there is one sinner, one prodigal, one lost soul in need of a Saviour, your court Salvationists will be spiritually strengthened and divinely motivated for their great task.

"'And you know, Tom,' the bishop concluded, 'when we as a church, and Christians as individuals, are moved by this same spirit and with the same conviction, we'll start changing the world as God intended we should.'"

I was nonplussed and a little embarrassed by such an unsolicited tribute, but as our fifteen-minute recess was already over, I had only time for a quick word of appreciation before we separated. We did not have contact again for several weeks, and then came a surprise phone call.

"This is Tom here," the caller announced. "You won't be seeing me in the courts any more as I am being transferred, but I felt I must phone to say that I will never forget you court people. In fact, I want to tell you that you have revitalized my faith. You did not know it. You did not set out to do it. But I have been conquered by your example."

Thank you, Tom, for this refreshing testimony. It makes me proud to be a Salvationist and a court worker. And it encourages all of us in this special, though arduous, service to which we believe God has called us.

I salute officers and lay Salvationists who quietly and devotedly serve in the Army's correctional, justice and multi-faceted social service agencies across Canada. For me it is a necessary reality shock prior to the comparatively secluded atmosphere of a scribe's life.

### *The Weariness and Wonder of Words*

Admittedly there is a keen sense of anticipation for Eva and me and our children when, following this temporary sojourn in Vancouver, we arrive in the congenial surroundings of Oakville, about 25 miles from territorial headquarters in Toronto. A few months earlier, of course, we had just returned to our homeland after more than 14 years in India. If Canada seemed next door to heaven, then Oakville had to be the front door.

Quickly settling down as a scribe, I become powerfully aware of the wonder and wearisomeness of words. Words are our stock in trade, whether used in original writing such as editorials and reporting assignments, or editing and proof-reading the manuscripts written by others.

Writing editorials are the most continuous challenge for an editor, I suppose. I develop my own system for reducing the possibility of staring at an empty sheet of typewriter paper, with mind just as empty and deadline passed.

Monday mornings I settle on my "Battle Lines" subject. Sometimes this is clearly defined by the issue date and a coinciding religious, historic, cultural or Salvation Army event. During the week, I jot down any relevant ideas or information that surfaces, and sharpen in my mind the direction the editorial will take.

Saturday mornings Eva and I do not sleep in too long. Instead, at about eight o'clock, and in relaxed clothing, we head to our favourite restaurant for a leisurely cooked breakfast. Then to the office, where thoughts move into high gear. I anticipate three hours of uninterrupted quietness and the relished opportunity not just to say something, but to say something that needs to be said, and to say it well. Words need to be chosen carefully, and then joined together with such flawless cohesion that the reader is persuasively convinced of the truth being declared.

It's fun, but hard work, and I can empathize with a heading which appeared before a freelance writer's contribution in *The Globe and Mail* some time ago. It said, "Between epiphanic moments of joy, one writer experiences intense stretches of straining against a head wind."

Some time ago James A. Mitchener's book, *The Novel*, captured my attention. Evidently autobiographical, it is an illuminating expose of a good writer's journey. He speaks of the rewriting which make just one paragraph a "creation of beauty: it's the basic unit of human thought, a format into which can be poured your most exalted conclusions, and also your most impassioned depictions of human relationships."

Of course, in the editorial department much time is spent in editing other's writing. There are many acceptable writers with good thoughts whose copy must be thoroughly edited for parallelism, coherence, integrity of verbs, respect for pronouns, elimination of superfluous adjectives and adverbs, factual accuracy and so on.

This is where the wearisomeness of words comes in. A paper like *The War Cry* has to be produced on time every week, holidays or sickness notwithstanding. One is under relentless pressure to prepare four, five or six pages with good copy, supported by good pictures and appealing layout. We are our own graphic designers! I often think of the linotype machines in the printing department downstairs as huge animals with voracious and insatiable appetites. We can never stop feeding them!

Before I begin writing editorials as editor-in-chief, I experiment with different types of writing. One style, which I continue for almost two years, linked humour and hyperbole to family experiences. Under the pen-name of Ed Scrybe the column was latterly called "Smile a Moment." It usually concluded with a spiritual punch line. One sample justifies inclusion here:

"I have to confess to leading my readers up the garden path. In my rambling ruminations I have frequently referred to - but only to—Sue, my superlative spouse! No doubt I have led you to believe that we are either newly-marrieds sharing the first flush of wedded bliss or, more likely, an over-the-hump Darby and Joan, living quiet, dignified lives, free from family cares and commitments.

"The truth is that Sue and I share our living accommodation with three boisterous offspring. Now I must be a little more specific and tell you that the Scrybe progeny are past the bouncing baby stage. Sue and I have survived 10,371 diaper changes, 216 hours of lost sleep, 4,357 bedtime stories and 21,483 mind-boggling questions. We are past the jam on the tablecloth, fingermarks on furniture, blithely destructive, enfant terrible stage; past the toddling, tumbling, make believe, kindergarten stage...

"Now we are at an era long-anticipated as relatively smooth sailing. But somehow we now find it has its own times of turbulence and tempest. Sally, our daughter, is almost seventeen and suffering—among other things—from boy-frienditis, Kris Kristoffersonitis and prolonged telephonitis. Unfortunately, she is also learning to drive.

"Steve and Scott are fourteen and 'mature eleven' respectively, and cheerfully regard our erstwhile haven of rest as an all-purpose recreational facility, dedicated particularly to sport and snack activity. With unabashed abandon they leave hockey equipment in the living room, soup dishes on the TV and pop bottles under the bed. They—and their friends—seem to monopolize every part of the house at the wrong time, except certain bathroom facilities that have soap and water as significant adjuncts.

"Inevitably, I look back with some nostalgia to the seemingly more ordered days of a decade ago when it was possible to reign as a kind of benign dictator. Domestic government now requires delicate dialogue and committee consultation.

"But frankly, these are more exciting days, and Sue and I are keen to live through them without regrets—especially so far as the younger folk are concerned. Perhaps that's why we feel strongly we must bring into our home life an atmosphere of wholesomeness, stability and purposeful living, which will have special meaning and value for our teenagers in these crucial years.

"'Who is sufficient for these things?' I read in my Bible this morning. Ed Scrybe? No way! 'My God is sufficient,' says the writer in conclusion. Because Sue and I believe this, we are striving more deeply to discover the mind of Christ so that our home life will be daily blessed with His guidance and grace."

It isn't difficult to write the Ed Scrybe articles. Most ideas just come from home life experiences. These years in Oakville are especially important, happy and memorable from a family point of view because we are all together, in contrast to the preceding and succeeding years when many miles and months (even years) separate us.

As a family we are fully committed to the Oakville Corps and a variety of activities. Howard, Graham and I all play in the band; Heather is a Sunday school teacher; and Eva is a Songster,

Home Leaguer, and League of Mercy worker. Eva, who is gifted with a winsome smile and infectious laugh, has always been a trusted critic of my writing. This is particularly appreciated and valued at the editorial office. Eva also gives volunteer service at the nearby Oakville municipal courthouse. Sometimes she will be called upon to translate for Hindi-speaking defendants.

### *An Unexpected Visitor*

I thought this midsummer day would be busy but quiet as I cleared some proofs from my desk at the Salvation Army's editorial office. Then the phone rang.

"Hi, this is Joe Slinger, *Toronto Star*, here," the voice began. "I would like to come out this afternoon and have a chat and see what you're doing there. Would that be possible?"

"No problem at all, come right over," I say, somewhat taken aback. I couldn't for the life of me imagine what idea he really had in the back of his mind.

Joe arrived early in the afternoon as promised, and in a deceptively casual way began to ask questions about the production of *The War Cry*, the editorial department's flagship paper. What were our motivations, challenges, hopes? He took time to look around the printing department (Triumph Press) downstairs, and to see a promotional slide presentation recently produced, before heading back to Toronto. All went well, but it was a little difficult to guess his inner thoughts, and what the final outcome would be.

It did not take long to find out, for the next day (August 11, 1982) his People Etc. column spelled it all out! Obviously, Joe Slinger knew quite a bit about *The War Cry* before he ever came out to Oakville. He started like this:

*"In his first editorial for the Salvation Army's weekly newspaper,* The War Cry, *Major Dudley Coles, who leaves next*

month after four years as editor-in-chief, mused about the appropriateness of the title of the editorial page—Battle Lines—in an age when men long to forget war.

"'The truth is, of course, that peace will always remain an elusive dream as long as we ignore the terrible disease of sin rampaging nations and men today. Evil must be fought with the same determination and singleness of purpose with which a soldier faces the enemy in wartime,' he wrote.

"Well might we envy The War Cry in this, the 98th year of its Canadian publication. It reports on a war that has clear battle lines, easily recognized victims and where the truth is the given truth of the Christian gospels. Listen to this snappy patter accompanying a promotional slide show: 'Many people complain all they hear and read is bad news. Probably a valid complaint. But some who are complaining haven't read the nations' good-news tabloid—the paper that probably reaches more people caught in bad news circumstances than any other publication...'"

Slinger then talked about a conviction that *The War Cry* was the world's most serene newspaper which came to him as he read the copies given him each week in a pub by a retired Salvation Army major. *"We were real newspapermen, cocky and sarcastic, we would joke about* The War Cry, *read bits aloud to one another over our beers. But something remained in my mind. No matter what,* The War Cry *held out hope... Tell me this news isn't as useful as anything else you read today."*

The well-known columnist finished with a few interesting paragraphs specifically about his visit to us.

*"Editor Coles knows his readership, knows that much of it is in hospital or in prison or in trouble of some kind. Somebody once wrote that these readers 'know the darkness that lurks in the midst of the bright lights; the pitiful weakness that masquerades as*

strength; the aching loneliness in the midst of crowds; the heartbreak not far below the surface of the empty laughter.'

"Yesterday, I went to visit Coles and tour his newsroom and the printing plant, a tidy, modern operation beside the Queen Elizabeth Way in Oakville. I went just because I wondered what he and it would be like. I found an efficient, soft-spoken, gray-haired man worried about how to keep young readers reading his paper. He has been fiddling around with the graphics, redesigning pages, trying to make it more appealing, more competitive.

"I could have had the same conversation with the editor of 'The Star', I thought. No matter what, we have a lot in common. The main difference is The War Cry *already knows what the news is. Here at* The Star *we have to wait and find out."*

### Facing Personal Challenges

My editorial duties take me on reporting assignments from Vancouver Island to Newfoundland, and in early months Eva and I are constantly in demand as missionary speakers. It is probably because I am pushing myself too much, and sensitively affected more than I realize by reverse culture shock, that I experience the most disturbing health problem of my life. This is less than a year after returning to Canada.

In the middle of the final meeting of a missionary seminar weekend in Newfoundland I suddenly experience the strangest feeling. As if a bolt of lightning has passed through me. With difficulty I conclude the service and share an ensuing tea fellowship. I am engulfed by an overwhelming sense of unease, and require some medication to get through the night and the flight home.

It is distressing to spend ten days in the psychiatric section of our local hospital, but clearly I am on the edge of a nervous breakdown and need careful observation. Soon, though, I am able to return to work, and put on an appearance of being fully recovered. In actual fact, for about three years I cannot go through a day without succumbing to feelings of unease, nameless fears and negative thoughts. During this period I almost withdraw from attending the Salvation Army's International College for Officers in London, England, due to a fear of flying that temporarily takes hold of me.

Evenings and nights are the most difficult. Looking back, I am sure my problems could have been lessened had I not been reluctant to take the tranquilizer medication prescribed. I am helped, however, by constantly calling on an armoury of positive thoughts (mostly Scripture) to dissipate the unbidden and undesired negative thoughts. Privately, I keep a little diary of my journey with God back to wellness. Examples:

*God's strength flows into me continually and is sufficient for my every need. By faith I see my fears, anxieties, tensions, unease, apprehensions, replaced by courage confidence, assurance, hopefulness and faith—and I give thanks, for so it will be, AMEN.*

*(Every prayer ends with a strong AMEN, "so be it!").*

*A series of 'God is Able's' concludes with Ephesians 3:20:*

*God is able to do exceedingly above all that ye ask or think...*

*Visualization of peaceful scenes, words (tranquility, serenity),*

*Songs, Let nothing disturb you... and Scripture, He leadeth me beside the still waters..., and quiet classical music.*

More than I can say, I am also aided by a strong and supportive wife. Eva is wonderful. Gradually, mental health and confidence return.

Reflecting on this experience, I have a tremendous sympathy for others who travel this same difficult road. Dr.Leslie Weatherhead, famed pastor of City Temple, London in World War II days suffered the experience of being nervously ill himself. He wrote sympathetically about those who are prey to anxious fears, who cannot get their minds off themselves, and for whom every demand fills them with foreboding. He would tell them that this feeling is illness, not cowardice; that millions have felt as they feel, that there is a way through this darkness, and light at the end of it.

My only other unpleasant health problem also happens in those Oakville years. This time I have an unexpected allergic reaction to penicillin. It takes ten days of special hospital care to straighten me out! Other than these experiences, however, I have enjoyed remarkably good health. Rarely have I missed a day's work or had so much as a consequential headache.

Through the last two years of our stay in Oakville, Eva and I share the private turmoil of deciding when to return to South Asia. Our personal prayer notebook of that period summarizes the struggle to match responsible parenthood with clear evidence that our services were needed overseas. The first request from International Headquarters comes in March 1980. "How soon can you return to the East?" we are asked. At that time Heather, Howard and Graham are still living at home and Graham, the youngest, is not quite seventeen. The prayer diary records: "Praying for guidance for ourselves and children. Have answered, available in 18 months—may the Lord continue to guide."

A year later the diary is reactivated as events reach their climax:

*"April 10, 1981: The General (Arnold Brown) makes two phone calls to territorial headquarters, again asking how soon we might be able to return to India. Difficult to give positive answer, wish request did not come so soon. We are willing, but are children ready? What is the Lord's will? Praying for clear guidance.*

*"April 18: This is Good Friday, it has been a week of upheaval, naturally; sang 738 again (Leave God to order all thy ways...and hope in him whate'er betide).*

*"April 19: We are in Halifax to report Congress and see General Arnold Brown. Eva and I had helpful interview with him.*

*"July 3: Prayed over letter expressing our willingness to prepare for September 1982 departure. We will now work in partnership with the Lord. Sang 488 (How can I better serve Thee, Lord... Lord for thy service fit me I plead). Have taken up Hindi lessons again!*

*"January, 1982: Have discussed future with Dr. Lee Fisher (Salvationist, psychologist and personal friend), and he has talked to Graham and is sending test (to ensure his coping ability). Also discussed with T.C. (Commissioner John Waldron)—both positive.*

*"May 7: Again asked to return to South Asia but this time to appointment which causes uncertainty and ambivalent feelings. After great heart searching and discussion have replied openly and frankly, and must now await IHQ decision.*

*"July 18: IHQ reply awaits us on return from furlough in West—'proposal shelved.'*

*"July 20: Receive telegram, 'Appointed to Sri Lanka as G.S.!' Came as shock; read words again of songs 738 and 488.*

*'July 23: Appointment announced and developments proceeding rapidly. May the Lord help us as we face all the difficult implications."*

Undoubtedly this was the most traumatic experience of our officership. The family upheaval affects us all more deeply than expected. We quickly begin the poignant task of helping the children find and furnish suitable apartment accommodation. And, difficult too, we all had to say goodbye to Pal, our loveable little dog, a mixture of poodle and something!

Separations are not new to us. It was, in fact, 23 years earlier, in June 1959, that we first said goodbye to Canada. And now our diary concludes: Sept.14: Depart from Toronto Airport. Tears before leaving and on plane.

## *REFLECTIONS*

The Salvation Army's structure does not allow its officers to choose their appointments. As in the armed forces, these are made by our leaders and allow a flexibility of response by administration to changing needs of its multi-faceted services not otherwise possible. We were supremely happy in our editorial appointment.

Increasingly today, appointments are made with a high level of sensitivity and pastoral care. Moves are also made with less frequency and more consultation.

Some of our happiest years as a family were spent in Oakville, fully sharing our children's teen years. We expected to see them safely through to adulthood. But it was not to be, and the thorough consultations prior to our return to South Asia have been outlined.

With the hindsight of years we now ask ourselves 'did we do the right thing? Was our decision the best?'

I still fall back on Romans 8:28: 'We know that in all things God works for good with those who love him' (Good News Bible). This same verse is quoted by Canon John Young of York Minster (U.K.), writing in a recent Salvation Army publication on the subject, 'Where is God when I make decisions.'

John Young says in part: "Note 'in all things'. God's relationship to us is dynamic, not static. He says: It doesn't matter where you are in life's maze, I am greater than your circumstances. Each day carries new possibilities and is always brimful of redemption."

Of course, we have not been alone in facing traumatic decisions. Renowned psychiatrist Paul Tournier has observed: "Even the happiest life is a constant struggle to face the problems it raises, the eternal and internal conflicts it arouses, which are the very stuff of life itself; a struggle to be true to oneself, to assume responsibility for one's own convictions..."

We have done that and God, who is no man's debtor, has graciously guarded and guided us as a family.

## CHAPTER 6: 1982 - 1987

## BLEMISHED PEARL OF THE ORIENT

### *The Trauma of Change*

The first South Asia Zonal Conference Eva and I attend is held in Bombay in September 1982, and timed immediately to follow great All India Centenary celebrations conducted by General and Mrs. Jarl Wahlstrom.

Zonal conferences, are usually conducted by the General, the Chief of the Staff and/or the International Secretary. Participating in these regional meetings are territorial leaders and chief secretaries. Lasting the better part of a week, with long days and full agendas, these conferences give a vital opportunity for international leaders to get to know national leaders personally. Unsurpassed fellowship includes more than happy camaraderie; it includes the mutual sharing of burdens and blessings, struggle and success.

We cannot forget the occasion because only seven weeks have passed since our placid family life in Canada had been shattered by a telegram from London advising that we are appointed to Sri Lanka where I am to be General Secretary. In a following letter we were invited to share in the centenary events in Bombay en route to Colombo. This would be a helpful introduction to our new responsibilities.

And of course it is. But we are drained of nervous and physical energy after some of the most traumatic days connected with departure preparation we have ever experienced in our officer-pilgrimage. Fortunately, the Centenary Congress revives our hearts and spirits as we renew contact with so many missionary and national friends whom we have not seen for almost nine years.

It does not take long for the chasm of absent years to diminish, and the sense of belonging to return. The re-enactment of the arrival of Booth-Tucker and his pioneer party of three at the Gateway to India 100 years earlier reminds us of a great heritage and mission once more to be shared. And attendance at the zonal conference introduces us to present day leaders in all the Indian territories as well as Pakistan, Bangladesh and Sri Lanka. We are also made sharply aware of current challenges in the region.

The week in Bombay has been beneficial personally in helping us to relax, catch our breath, and gain afresh the stabilizing assurance of God's guiding hand upon us. Soon we are flying down the south-west coast of India towards Sri Lanka where a new life adventure awaits discovery. Little do we know that within a year we will be assuming territorial leadership. Nor do we know that almost simultaneously, an ethnic conflict will break out brutalizing the nation and changing for decades the tranquil beauty of this lovely island.

A 14$^{th}$ century Italian friar said that Ceylon, as it was then known, is but 40 miles from Paradise. He can't be far from the truth in many ways, for Sri Lanka—literally resplendent island—is renowned for gems, spices and tea. It enjoys an extravagance of flora and fauna garlanded by pristine beaches glittering under a tropical sky. Lying almost on the Equator, it seems to have two seasons—hot and hotter. While there is a monsoon season, rain falls more generally through the year, thus adding to the island's humidity.

Sri Lanka is about the size of New Brunswick and has a population almost two-thirds that of Canada. Seventy percent of the people are Sinhalese, and almost all of these are Buddhists who proudly claim an unbroken history and civilization dating back to the sixth century B.C. They are an Aryan people and, unusual for Buddhist societies, have many castes. Other ethnic groups are Tamils (mainly Hindu) 20%, and Moors (Muslim) 6%. Just over 7% of the population are Christian and 90% of these are Roman Catholic.

While there had been some incidents of racial violence before our arrival, Sri Lanka was an example of a Third World nation making remarkable progress on the road to economic stability and social enhancement. I find a stimulating introduction to "Sri Lanka's Development Thrust" in reading a book with that title written by Mallory E. Wijesinghe. Alongside many important business responsibilities, Mallory has for many years chaired The Salvation Army's Colombo Advisory Board. How grateful we are to have his knowledgeable and influential support.

For the first nine months in Sri Lanka Eva and I happily support Colonel and Mrs. William Perera, the first national officers to assume territorial leadership. The Colonel, tall and slim, has been well-trained by his predecessor in office, the then Commissioner Eva Burrows, and also has the support of a petite and gracious wife. Both are fluent in English and bring dignity and friendliness to their leadership roles. They are always most kind to Eva and me and give us opportunity for orientation travels from Colombo on the west coast to Batticaloa in the east, Jaffna in the north and Galle in the south.

These early months in Sri Lanka include the exciting visit of General and Mrs. Jarl Wahlstrom for centenary celebrations. We are able to learn all the intricacies of planning and preparation that lie behind such occasions. Too quickly the historic gatherings become history, but the emotional exhilaration and spiritual enrichment long remain.

On the domestic side, we quickly settle in to our modestly furnished but comfortable home in Bambalapitiya. It is situated down a little lane between busy Galle Road and the sea on the south-west side of Colombo. We also quickly learn to love Alice, whose caring ministrations in the home over a period of almost thirty years to a succession of missionary leaders, wins the lasting affection and unbounded appreciation of us all.

General Frederick Coutts refers to Alice in his biography of Commissioner Gladys Calliss, an Australian officer who gave territorial leadership in 1973 after many years of notable service in Indonesia. He writes:

> *"Any domestic title would be far too inadequate a description for one who had served successive territorial commanders over many years. She may not have carried any official rank but no money would have bought the personal service given daily—virtually hourly—by the Sinhalese Alice."*

When we arrive at 3 St. Alban's Place, we are greeted by Alice, little more than four-feet tall, barely 76 pounds in weight and close to 70 years in age. Still sprightly, Alice is definitely in charge of household affairs! We quickly discover what a boon she will be to us in our ministry.

### *An Inauspicious Beginning*

The year 1983 will long be remembered. Not because we assume command of the territory. More significantly it marks the eruption of island-wide violence between Sinhala Buddhists and Tamil Hindus. Regrettably the violence continues into this first decade of a new century which the United Nations has declared a Decade for the Culture of Peace and Non-Violence.

It is just nine months after our arrival in Sri Lanka that Eva and I slip out of the house at dawn on that first day of July and drive to the Khan Clock Tower in the Pettah area of downtown

Colombo. It is our installation day. We want to absorb something of the spirit of Captain William Gladwin who stood on this spot 100 years earlier and all alone proclaimed the saving grace of Jesus Christ.

It is hardly an encouraging beginning to The Salvation Army's arrival in the Ceylon of 1883. In fact *The Times* of Ceylon editorialized, "We decline to lend the smallest aid to any of (Captain Gladwin's) blasphemous proceedings. We most sincerely trust that no European or native will countenance these coarse, vulgar, degrading exhibitions of fanaticism by their presence."

The *Ceylon News*, a little more temperate, comments: "Mr. Gladwin, the fore-runner of The Salvation Army which is about to invade Ceylon, and by a process at once novel and queer, to convert the godless heathen and rouse the apathetic Christian, has...arrived in Ceylon... We do not see why Mr. Gladwin and his associates in arms should not be left to themselves..."

But Bishop J.B. Lightfoot is one of those who made the most accurate assessment. He said, "The Salvation Army has at least recalled us to the lost ideal of the work of the Church, the universal compulsion of the souls of men." William Booth, of course, was a realist. When he spoke of 'saving souls' he meant making persons whole in the physical, spiritual and social dimensions of life.

As Eva and I stand at Khan Clock we survey the early morning activity of shopkeepers and outdoor market vendors preparing for a busy day. We praise God for the rich blessing showered upon his Army through the intervening years. We would now assume responsibility for a Movement known and respected throughout the island for what President J.R. Jayewardene described as "missionary zeal, exemplary dedication...and unostentatious charity."

Before returning to headquarters for a busy round of installation events to be conducted by Commissioner Inez Newberry, we pray together. "Help us Lord," we say, "to worthily follow the steps of pioneers and predecessors as we march Sri Lankan Salvationists into their second century of divinely-blessed service."

Sri Lankans are renowned for the gorgeous orchid garlands, beautiful decorations and traditional courtesies which are a part of special occasions. These all add to our installation event shared with well-wishers from many church and community groups.

I think it might be helpful to comment at this time regarding our assuming command after a period of national leadership. "To some, this might appear a backward step," I acknowledge. "But let us remember that The Salvation Army is an international Movement, and it is essential that its leadership continue to have an opportunity for international experience." I point out that in my home territory just prior to our South Asia return, we had served under an American territorial commander, a British chief secretary, and an Australian financial secretary!

Before concluding on a spiritual note of remembering the rich heritage bequeathed to us and resolving to "stir up our own God-given gifts," I also acknowledge the needed support of two very special people. One would be the national general secretary, Major Vincent Perera, "whose long experience and wise counsel will be imperative and valued," and secondly my wife, "about whom I will at this moment simply echo Churchill's succinct but far from adequate words, 'I married, and lived happily ever after.'" Little did I imagine that within a few short weeks the inadequacy of my words about Eva would be superbly demonstrated.

I believe my first order of business as territorial leader should be to meet with all our island officers at our Hikkaduwa conference centre and chart a strategy for the immediate future.

With keen anticipation, Eva and I travel on the Sunday night, planning to spend Monday in necessary on-the-spot final preparations for the officers' arrival the following day. The two-hour drive southward down the coastal Galle Road to Hikkaduwa is delightful, with many breathtaking vistas of sand and sea, palm trees and fishing boats. Hikkaduwa itself is a little village just twenty minutes from the historic town of Galle. The area has developed as a tourist resort. The conference centre has special attraction to Salvationists as the ancestral home of Arnolis Weerasooriya, the first Sri Lankan to join Gladwin's band of courageous pioneers.

But on Monday an unexpected message is sent from a nearby hotel asking me to phone headquarters immediately. Reluctantly the General Secretary, Major Vincent Perera, advises me that communal violence on an unprecedented scale had broken out and is quickly spreading throughout the island. The officers 'retreat' must be cancelled. He wonders if Eva and I would prefer to stay in the south for the time being. I assure him we would rather close up the centre and return to Colombo as quickly as possible. Then the phone line disconnects.

Excerpts of diary notes made at the time may not have reflective balance but they do provide a vivid replay of instinctive reactions and emotional responses in the midst of turmoil and tension. Here are some extracts:

*"Tuesday. Local police station advise us to call at each police station along the way before proceeding further. There is a tense atmosphere on route and soon we enter the curfew area and have to get passes to continue. We count more than 200 burned shops, businesses and homes before reaching Dehiwela in Colombo's outskirts where we have two institutions. Find matron has hidden 65 refugees in an empty bungalow.*

"They are in great danger and I rush to the police station to seek help. Police are too busy. I hear them discussing what to do with mutilated bodies. Finally, though, they do send some transport and we use our own vehicles. On the way to refugee camp with frightened people who hide under seats, our vehicles face threatening mobs. Burned buses and cars are strewn everywhere...Young men are pulling shingles from rooftops before setting houses on fire.

"Heart-stopping moments as we also help in the removal of people hiding in neighbouring homes. Rush to police station to obtain curfew pass. Then journey on to Colombo and begin tour of our six local institutions all of which have Tamil and Sinhala residents. Security of Tamils is our most serious problem.

"Wednesday. Make early morning phone call to all our institutions. All safe. Some training college cadets have been transferred to our 'Haven' home nearby—this is probably safer. Matron of our Rajagiriya boys' home is Tamil and we visit her to check the situation. She is a widow, and brave. Some of our Sinhala people have courageously taken in Tamil refugees to hide. Bless them.

"Thursday. Armed patrols on street now very strict. Constantly stopped and, while one serviceman points rifle at my heart, the other checks curfew pass. Institutions still OK but receiving threatening phone calls and messages. On evening visit I call all residents together and give stern warning to keep doors locked, and remain out of sight. Pray at each institution for safety and peace of occupants.

"Friday. Went to meeting called by government, and Salvation Army is allocated a refugee camp to serve. We will prepare daily soup for 2,000 people. Major Perera (G.S.) and I get caught in Pettah crossfire as military and *police flush out unknown assailants and looters. Some scary moments as we zig-zag our way on foot through debris-filled streets, hardly knowing which way to go.*

"Some 400 shops have been burned or seriously damaged in this area. *False rumours have heightened tension today and patrols are particularly edgy on streets after dark. We drive cautiously. Hostel matrons are under great strain, as are all others, and threats continue directly and by phone. Nerve-wracking. Eva and I continue to make rounds, reassuring residents and staffs, and offering prayers.*

*"Saturday. Make three-hour journey with G.S. and a divisional officer to renowned hill-station town of Kandy to check on relief work being undertaken and general situation. On return had harrowing experience of van being surrounded. But on seeing armed policeman (we had picked him up just two minutes earlier!) the intending attackers change their minds. Two missionary officers en route from Colombo airport to headquarters have similar experience and cannot sleep all night as their minds relive the frightening moments.*

*"Sunday. Curfew continues without a break all weekend so usual Sunday services are cancelled. Under the direction of Eva and Mrs. Major Maureen Perera the refugee clothing distribution starts. Thank goodness we have clothing stored for such emergencies and needs. It is a slow business as hundreds of people surround our vans desperate for a change of clothing. Soup is served from one van and clothing from the other three.*

It is tiring, non-stop work. Camp leaders give us several bolts of cloth and ask that we make 400 sarongs. The request is met in two days with the assistance of our Ladies Hostel women.

How much longer will this tense atmosphere continue, we wonder?"

So the diary continues describing the great work done in refugee camps with soup and clothing distribution, an infinite variety of personal needs being met, and the secret evacuation of endangered residents of our institutions to their home areas. In all this, Major and Mrs. Perera, Sinhala officers, demonstrated unbiased concern for the suffering, and tireless initiative in organizing and sustaining many of the Army's relief programs.

Let one story represent the many that could be told of these first days of massive national violence. At the end of the first week we hear that the General Secretary of the Bible Society, a Tamil, is in hiding in his home above the society's office, and is in need of food. With our permit we set out during a curfew period and, after checking all is clear around the Bible Society building, enter the compound. A head peeps through the curtain of an upstairs window and soon a side door is cautiously opened—and quickly bolted behind us.

With the general secretary and his wife are their daughter and son-in-law and their children. The son-in-law who is head of the Every Home Crusade office in downtown Colombo has escaped with his family after having had his house ransacked and all the Crusade vehicles burned. He is very upset and fearful.

These fine Christian evangelists gratefully accept the food we have brought, and briefly but vividly describe the harrowing days they have just passed through. We then share a time of spiritual fellowship. We read God's Word, sing some hymns and choruses of encouragement, and pray together. In these moments of continuing heartache and fearful uncertainty, the atmosphere of Christian love and hope is powerful and we sense the mystical presence of our Lord in a remarkable way. After promising to undertake one or two needed requests, we quietly and cautiously slip away. A hallowed memory indeed.

To continue to record all the tense moments of the next five years of our stay in Sri Lanka would become repetitious. Colombo does not return to complete normalcy. Military searching of cars and personal belongings continues, and every now and then there are tragic bombing incidents, curfews and emergency situations. Visiting a hospital on one occasion shortly after a bomb 'incident' that killed or injured 300 people, I hear a desperate cry of "Help, help, will someone help me?" It is a young man, bloodied and blinded by the blast. "What can we do for you?" I ask. "Please hold my hand," was the poignant reply. I am glad to offer this reassuring gesture to the injured man who is still in severe shock.

Outside of Colombo, our visits to the Jaffna area of the north and the Batticaloa area of the East become increasingly difficult and dangerous, and often impossible. And yet it is so necessary to keep in touch with our people and assure them of our continuing support and prayers, and see that they receive necessary monthly grants.

Through all these experiences I learn a lot about myself. I am not a naturally courageous person with tremendous reserves of nervous energy. In fact, it is often necessary to act courageously even though inwardly fearful. Sometimes I long for the tension to diminish.

Fortunately, there are a number of ways this can be handled. Firstly, of course, fear faced is fear conquered, and the determination to press on in spite of fear cultivates personal confidence and control. Then Eva is always a great support and strong partner, and our home always a haven of peace and harmony where depleted reserves of mental, physical and emotional energy are restored. The loving and concerned ministrations of Alice aid this, as does a good night's sleep. We are both fortunate in usually managing to sleep well.

I have always found walking a helpful means of relaxation and fitness, so necessary at this time. Of great help, too, is the privilege given missionaries of membership in the Colombo Swimming Club. We use this to great advantage. Tennis is also a regular early Saturday morning activity. I particularly remember, however, the benefit received from late night swims at the club during curfew days. We are given special permission to use the pool, and the restorative effect of quiet water exercise in the stillness of a warm tropical evening under a star-lit sky is magical.

Somewhere I read that when a Christian gets to the end of his rope he ties a knot and hangs on. How often God allows us to get to the 'end of our resources,' but amazingly never beyond! Always strength is given to hang on. And relief has come!

Because the tranquility of our Island-paradise had been so tragically shattered I issue a special call to a ministry of reconciliation. Coinciding with the United Nations designated International Year of Peace, we prepare a peace poster printed in Sinhala, Tamil and English that dramatically announces, "Want peace—make peace. Jesus said, 'Blessed are the peacemakers.'" The Ceylon Bible Society helps us produce and finance the posters that we aim to have hung in every Salvationist home in the island—and many others.

On a designated Sunday our congregations are encouraged to hold a special service in which members individually sign a peace pledge. They are then given an attractively-designed gold and blue card with a dove superimposed on a map of Sri Lanka, and the word 'peace' in three languages forming a background. The pledge, printed inside, is simple: 'I promise, with God's help, to be a peacemaker—in my home, corps and community. I will try to live up to the highest standards of Christian conduct under all circumstances and in all situations.' Yes, the pledge is simple, but one which it is desirable to have our racially-divided Salvationists affirm.

### Getting on with Life Amid the Strife

In spite of the underlying national problems it is necessary to get on with life, and to move forward in our witness, evangelism and service. Sri Lankans are lovely people and it is a constant joy to share in developing programs and projects that will enhance the effectiveness of the Army's ministry. The Army uniform is recognized and admired by President and peasant, business-man and bus driver.

Sunshine House and Hope House are two projects opened during our stay. Sunshine House, built in the same compound as The Haven (renowned for its many decades of service to unmarried mothers and abandoned children), is set up at the request of the government to accommodate up to fifty young women remand prisoners. What stories the matron can tell of her caring ministry!

Hope House is built on the former territorial headquarters building site and designed to teach handicapped people the skills necessary for self-support and independent living. My successors have notably enhanced the programs administered by this highly visible building.

We also felt that child care is an area of fast-growing need where, at little cost but mutual benefit to corps and community, The Salvation Army can make a notable contribution. We send a number of women officers on special courses, and centres attached to carefully-chosen corps are progressively prepared to open this ministry. It is encouraging to see how wisely and well our successors have established this practical community service.

It is always difficult to judge the advancement of corps work and spiritual ministry. I wish we could see clearer evidence of positive progress in this area. Certainly special attention is given to the further training of departmental and divisional leaders through quarterly meetings and greater discussion. We start our leadership with a hundred-day assessment period. Each corps is visited and a questionnaire completed which seeks to judge the present spiritual condition of the officer and his corps people. The summarized results are studied and efforts made to use the information to better plan future strategy.

Visits to up-country corps at weekends are always a joy, even when journeys are hot and tiresome. Conducting meetings in the Rambukkana area, for instance, means leaving Colombo at dawn and travelling winding and pot-holed roads for a couple of hours to the divisional centre. There we pick up the divisional leaders and journey on narrow and often unpaved roads until the vehicle can take us no further. Then, carrying Bibles and umbrellas we walk along the bundhs (small embankments) that separate lush green paddy fields.

Eventually we spy amidst a clump of palm trees the little Army hall of, say, Siyambalangamuya, and joyful Salvationists waiting to greet us. Civil unrest notwithstanding, there is tranquil beauty and gracious hospitality throughout our short stay at such village corps. It is a privilege to offer a message of simple Christian practicality.

There is certainly a great need for Christians (missionary and national) to understand the culture in which they live and witness. There are dangers (even arrogance) in preaching the gospel of Jesus Christ if we do not have at least a basic understanding of Buddhism, for instance.

To illustrate, Christians are partial to John 3:16 when sharing their faith. But the prospect of eternal life in the verse is anathema to the Buddhist whose ultimate goal is 'nirvana'—nothingness. Christians must not give the impression that 'eternal life' refers merely to prolongation of life. It is a different quality of life, the divine life granted to believers.

There is much that the Christian can respect in Buddhism. There is elimination of unlawful desires and materialism; the urge to follow the good life (according to the Eightfold Path and the Five Precepts); the pursuit of world peace, the sacredness of all things and the practise of the devotional life.

But it is a self-salvation, and there are practices that some Christians tend to observe—to their peril. Astrology is one such, and even government departments will seek astrological advice as to when to mark a special occasion. Witchcraft is another, and this can be used for most undesirable purposes. All people need to know the forgiveness and peace that only Christ can give.

A problem, not linked to Buddhism, but prevalent in Sri Lanka as in many other parts of the world has to do with sexual laxity. The difficulty for us is compounded when our own people are involved. I think my most difficult task as a leader was to discipline officers found guilty of sexual offences. Rumours abound in Sri Lanka, but rarely can they be authenticated.

I will never forget the sleepless nights and heart-searching which precede my dismissal of two officers on one occasion. The officer-wife of one has to be released at the same time, though without blame. They are intelligent, hard-working young officers who speak English fluently, and clearly would make a valued contribution to the future life of the territory. The man frankly admits guilt. He is astounded, though, when I tell him my decision. "But," he says, "there are other officers just as guilty as me, but they don't admit it. Are you going to punish an honest officer?" For me the problem is that no one can be pronounced guilty on the basis of rumour—sexual misconduct has to be proved or admitted. In this case there is both proof and admission.

Living the authentic Christian life in a non-Christian environment is difficult, and we can only stand in awe of the many lovely Sri Lankans who worthily exemplify Salvationism.

~~~ ~~~ ~~~

Amidst the endless variety of experiences each day brings, we never forget our children, ten thousand miles away. We miss them greatly and recognize how important these years are for young people as they move from late teens into early twenties. How are our children doing, and how do they feel about our absence? Correspondence is a vital form of continuing family communication. (Phoning is expensive for us, and in pre-satellite days, unreliable. Calls are pre-booked, and made from special phone centres). Here is one extract from a letter we send to Heather, Howard and Graham in Canada:

"Graham won't mind me saying that we thought he gave a very thoughtful, balanced and perceptive reply to the question of our return to Sri Lanka again, after anticipated furlough. He then refers to his friend going into The Salvation Army training college and makes the comment (no doubt with tongue in cheek) 'stupid guy!' And when we think of the costliness of our service over the past 30 years we have to say true, absolutely true—unless one is aware of a divine call which is compelling and irresistible. 'Don't go into the ministry if you can stay out,' said Bishop Cushman to a young prospective candidate; and then he added, 'I hope you can't stay out!'

"Certainly this was Mum's experience, and mine, too! We were aware of 'the divine pursuit'—your grandfather wrote a tone poem for Army bands based on the epic poem of Francis Thompson with this name. It speaks of the majestic, untiring, persistent footsteps of the 'Master of Men' calling us to follow Him.

"To know this compulsive call—beyond intellectual argument yet not requiring abdication of intelligent reasoning—is to have an anchor that holds one steady in all the storms ensuing years will inevitably bring. G. Campbell Morgan, (renowned Methodist preacher and writer of my early years) felt so strongly about 'God's choosing, calling and equipping' that he never asked men to enter the Christian ministry. 'He needs to know that it is God who set him on this journey and that he dare not turn back. This conviction can sustain a man in his high calling when everything else fails him.'

"Well, I guess that's been quite a sermon, but it's good for me sometimes to clarify and share something which is very personal and tremendously significant to decisions we make—decisions which have direct and far-reaching family consequences."

Of course, it is this compelling sense of God's will and guidance that brought Eva and me to Sri Lanka after nine extremely happy years in Canada. And again it is this compelling sense of guidance that brings peace and assurance to our hearts when another unexpected telegram arrives from London. From September 1, 1987, we are to assume leadership of the South Asia Department at International Headquarters.

## *REFLECTIONS*

There is a little inconsistency in our appointment to Sri Lanka. For eighteen months we had been preparing to go to India. Apparently International Headquarters needed to respond to an emergency health breakdown related to our predecessors. However, we are still a part of the South Asia region, and Romans 8:28 is still our valid anchor.

The decisions made in four of the next five years did not concern our future. Rather they were decisions we made affecting our territorial officers and staffs, our community involvements, and the growth, integrity and effectiveness of the Salvation Army's varied ministries.

Unexpected civil strife nationwide provided an opportunity for the Army to be seen at its best, fully committed to any relief, rehabilitation and reconstruction assistance the government requested. Western embassies make arrangements for the evacuation of missionary wives and children, if desired. None of ours leave the Island.

"This is true JOY in life," wrote George Bernard Shaw, "the being used for a purpose recognized by ourself as a mighty one." Ours is! We also knew that our leadership abilities are being tested and stretched.

## Chapter 7: 1987 - 1991

## A Full Cup in London

### *Roles and Goals*

Arrival at International Headquarters on famed Queen Victoria Street in the City of London, and within sight of St. Paul's Cathedral had, for Eva and me, unmatched significance.

We wore, for the first time, the distinctive trim of commissioners, and knew that we were now among 70 or 80 of that privileged rank among an officer force of about 25,000 world-wide. This is not the place to argue for, or against, the Army's rank system. Suffice to say that it has always been seen as a necessary part of a quasi-military structure, even though promotions can occasionally cause hurts and disappointment.

However, I particularly remembered some words of General Wilfred Kitching that fastened to the memory of a young and impressionable probationary lieutenant. Spoken at an officers' council in Toronto shortly after his election, the world leader said, "It takes a steady hand to carry a full cup."

Inseparably linked to great privilege is great responsibility. No one can hold high office in any Christian organization without being aware that divine judgement accompanies divine blessing. Sensitive to God's grace, we remember that a good measure of humility must parallel such recognition.

It is wise, also, to carry privilege and position lightly, knowing, as Shakespeare said, that "all the world's a stage." Having made our entry into a high profile scene, we will similarly and quickly, make our exit. Most likely this is our last appointment, retirement is just three-and-a-half years away.

From the first day in office, then, I understand that I must grasp the intricacies of my role thoroughly and fulfill it competently. I must also set some clear goals that, few but significant, will be of lasting benefit to the area of the world for which I have particular responsibility. Eva, in her new role as assistant secretary for women's organizations, South Asia, faces similar challenges.

For me, these soon come into sharp focus following a discussion with my predecessor in office, Commissioner David Durman, the reading of briefs and priority documentation, and an initial visit to South Asia in my new role as international secretary for South Asia.

Firstly, and unquestionably, a carefully-developed strategy for the future of The Salvation Army in India is needed. Heightened co-operation and co-ordination between the five separate territorial commands is essential. This is also in the General's mind as a result of personal observations and contacts.

The Army's world leader instructs me to set up an India Strategy Commission. The Salvation Army in India (representing one-seventh of the movement's world-wide officer-force) tends to be responding too sluggishly to external changes and internal crises.

The Army in India faces sharply diminished expatriate leadership support, the retirement of outstanding national leaders and increasing economic and financial restraints. Within the sub-continent a resurgence of militant Hinduism, government restrictions and caste conflicts, all aggravate the situation.

Thirty years have passed since Eva and I first arrived in India, and the changes, particularly in cities, startle us. Western style buildings have mushroomed, as have scooters and computers. Traffic and people choke roads more than ever before. Urban areas have burgeoned with pavement dwellers and squalid slums, open drains and ever-present garbage. There seems to be a general inability to cope with a fast-multiplying population and its basic needs. Many buildings reveal only the vestiges of a former glory. Bribery and corruption appear more prevalent. Exorbitant amounts of time and energy are expended to accomplish anything.

Indian Salvationists cannot be blamed for succumbing in some measure to the general malaise. Financial resources (including grants from London) are inadequate. The missionary presence is severely curtailed, reduced from well over a hundred in the 1960s to a handful 20 years later. Replacement national leaders are thrust into positions of high responsibility with insufficient training or preparation.

But to return to the commission. Preliminary studies occupy a year. They begin with extensive surveys touching every strata of Army life, and conclude with fine-tuning the commission's agenda, terms of reference and logistics. Crucial is the selection of nine commission members. Events prove that the choice of chairman is divinely-inspired. Lieut.-Colonel (Dr.) Paul du Plessis guides his commission members through their thorough investigations with consummate skill. The 200-page report—reduced to a 20-page summary by the General herself, and to a Churchillian-style one page summary by the chairman—is a masterly accomplishment. It sets the direction for the Army's work into the $21^{st}$ century.

Commission recommendations will not solve every problem. But implementation has clearly given a new unity of direction to the five territories involved, and brought about a remarkable integration of purpose and planning. A Conference of Indian Leaders (COIL) meets annually. It gives guidance to a national office as well as to inter-territorial offices that co-ordinate such specialized ministry areas as leadership training, human resources and health services. Progress continues, and there is satisfaction in seeing a goal so fully realized.

Another goal set at the beginning of my tenure as international secretary, is to get at least one missionary couple into India who can help bridge the gap caused by the retirement of outstanding national leaders. We need someone who knows India and who can work effectively with associate India territorial commanders in implementing Strategy Commission recommendations. Who better than the chairman of that body? But only a miracle can achieve such a dream—visas for non-Indians are almost impossible to obtain. We steadily tackle all the problems for two years and then, incredibly, the miracle happens. Another goal wonderfully fulfilled, with immeasurable long-term benefit to the Salvation Army in India.

~~~ ~~~ ~~~

An international secretary has numerous roles not directly related to zonal responsibilities. Membership of finance, projects and literature councils have some bearing, but to be involved in the evolution of a restructured I.H.Q. is a time-consuming, yet fascinating experience.

The restructuring had two directions. 'International' headquarters really had its genesis when a 'foreign office' was opened to better administer a Salvation Army leap-frogging around the world in a manner little imagined when it began as 'The Christian Mission' in 1865.

Practical and historic links inevitably, and almost inextricably, bind I.H.Q. and the Army in Great Britain together. Separation of the two is long overdue. Many serious and determined attempts to address the gigantic task of dismantling the existing structure result in significant progress. But the final accomplishment of this enormously complicated procedure is an historic achievements of General Eva Burrows' tenure of office. Colonel John Larsson (later General) is its 'chief architect.'

Simultaneously, opportunity arises to restructure international headquarters itself so that more attention will be given, within a smaller but more focused administration, to guiding strategies, policies and plans. Through the expertise of functional as well as geographic departments, a new pattern of leadership will result in less controlling and more facilitating.

The principal forum for strategy planning under the restructured I.H.Q., which comes into being on November 1, 1990, is the International Management Council. It is a privilege to be a founding member.

Keenly anticipated and always memorable occasions are international conferences of world leaders which usually take place every three years or so. For a number of years now wives, who also hold senior leadership roles, have shared equally with their husbands and other women leaders.

Few can be more contrasting than two we shared - one in the somewhat stringent Berlin of iron curtain days, and the other at Lake Arrowhead, in Southern California, U.S.A. General and Mrs. Jarl Wahlstrom, Finnish leaders of quiet grace and warm friendliness, lead the first occasion. General Eva Burrows, the first woman General since Evangeline Booth (half a century earlier), brings an Australian openness, energy and effervescence to the second.

Sharing leadership in Berlin is Chief of the Staff Commissioner Caughey Gauntlett (who, appropriately, has a strong European background and linguistic abilities). In Lake Arrowhead, Chief of the Staff Commissioner Ronald Cox, an unflappable Englishman of buoyant spirit and wide Africa experience, supports General Burrows.

An indescribable warmth permeates these conferences and the relationship existing between world leaders. Our cultural backgrounds and personal characteristics vary, but unitedly we share an affinity that brings about an immediate bonding. There are problems and heartaches within the Army, of course, but nothing undermines the strong comradeship developed in a shared experience, a joyous faith, evangelistic spirit, compassionate heart and disciplined lifestyle.

In September 1988, the Americans host us with unsurpassed kindness and generosity at Lake Arrowhead, often called the jewel of the San Bernadino mountains of southern California. What an experience to move from the hustle and bustle of big cities, and the pressures of leadership, to the quiet seclusion and quaint charm of this Alpine village setting!

But we do not meet for a holiday get-together with relaxed conference agenda and optional attendance! Except for the Saturday public welcome at the Crystal Cathedral and Sunday worship, most of the nine days are spent in working sessions. Many of the 26 sessions are intense and long. Inevitable difficulties arise in obtaining consensus when sharing discussions with 115 leaders representing 90 countries and territories of the Army world. How much we have to learn from each other! Through it all prevails a unity that would make the United Nations envious.

General Eva Burrows quickly reminds us of the Founder's warning that the Army 'should beware of three dangers: stagnation, secularization, self-satisfaction.' How easy to become rigid and inflexible, cushioned by regulation and tradition! How easy to compromise with the materialistic spirit of our present age, and to diminish the sacrifice still essential to Christ-like ministry! How easy to succumb to self-congratulation and plaudits while ignoring justified criticism!

So the General urges us to tackle the hard questions and courageously seek new directions and solutions. I think we do, as our discussions move from divorce to doctrine, ranks to relationships, human rights and moral issues to local officers and candidateship. We talk about the perplexities of maintaining our internationalism despite government and legal restrictions, and the sensitivity necessary to balance social concern and spiritual ministry.

But frankly, my sharpest and most moving memories are of the Berlin leaders' conference a few years earlier. In this more austere setting we feel strangely warmed by our proximity to East Berlin and a struggling church facing the tremendous pressures and difficulties of a Marxist-Socialist state. Little do we imagine the staggering events so soon to take place!

Our itinerary includes an indelibly remembered five-hour visit to East Berlin. What consternation three busloads of uniformed Salvationists make at Checkpoint Charlie! What feelings of reluctance as we temporarily surrender our passports! We meet the bishop of evangelical churches and learn of some of the restrictions under which he and his parishioners live and work. Not only do we pray the Lord's Prayer (in 20 languages) at his request, but we also sing the Founder's song with its reminder of 'the whole world redeeming.'

But equally moving are final moments with our East German bus guide who accompanies us throughout our journeys behind the 'Iron Curtain.' Before leaving us at Checkpoint Charlie she asks that we sing Luther's magnificent hymn, "A mighty fortress is our God." And we do, with deep respect for our friends in Christ beyond the wall.

## *The Burden of Leadership*

Meetings of the General's Advisory Council, always highly significant, often involve leadership decisions at the highest level. (I am privileged to be a member of this body for its 1000th meeting.) Proposed appointments are not always approved unanimously. There is consternation among some members of the council on one occasion as we review the career records of an officer the General is proposing for territorial leadership in South Asia.

The General has agreed to my personal recommendation, and now I vigorously defend the proposal on her behalf. No easy task. Some council members are legitimately concerned to maintain the highest traditions of holy living and life-long integrity in Army leadership. They cannot endorse someone whose career has included disciplinary action and negative appraisal. Others, while recognizing weaknesses, past or present, nevertheless see the great strengths and special situational considerations that justify approval.

Advisory Council recommendations are returned to the General who then proceeds with implementation. On rare occasions the General disagrees with her advisory council's recommendation, and she will convey her reasons for a contrary decision personally.

We hold weekly meetings of the Overseas Council, the Chief of the Staff's business meeting and the General's business meeting. The five I.S.s (international secretaries), representing different areas of the world, provide the 'gateway' through which territorial leaders within their regions seek direction and advice from international headquarters. Decisions and action are facilitated through these weekly IHQ business meetings.

~~~ ~~~ ~~~

The Overseas Service Council comprises the five zonal I.S.s (to which three functional I.S.s—administration, finance and resources—are latterly added). Each I.S. rotates as chairman, while under-secretaries present matters for discussion. The Under-Secretaries (chief assistants to international secretaries) enter the boardroom only to present the business of his or her region. One is a grandson of General Bramwell Booth whose large portrait dominated a wall. The Army's second General, who laid the foundations of the Movement's governing principles with remarkable astuteness, appears to be listening to our deliberations with high expectations and benevolent goodwill.

Sharing our business in this way results in undoubted benefits. As an international group (British, American, Canadian, Australian and Danish, for instance) we bring our own perspectives and experience to each discussion. Wider representation, with Asian, African and South American participants, is now normal.

One morning, my competent under-secretary, Lieut.-Colonel Ron Johnson, brought to the table the case of a Canadian officer-couple who had applied for missionary service, and accepted an appointment in Sri Lanka. They had been approved at an earlier meeting, and the South Asia Department (for which I was responsible) was responsible for final preparation, including the travelling arrangements.

Considerable consternation arises when, after a night in England en route, they suddenly change their minds and decide to return home. The couple convey their decision to me personally in a long conversation. I also have them share their feelings with our medical advisor and an experienced counsellor. Contact is urgently made with the sending and receiving territories, as well as the Chief of the Staff.

Now the Overseas Service Council wants a lot of questions answered before supporting any recommendation to send them home. The receiving territory, while dismayed at the last minute possibility of being deprived of greatly needed reinforcements, does not want an even more serious problem some time after arrival. The I.S. for the Americas and Caribbean conveys the unhappiness of the home territory and wants to know where the screening and preparation process has failed.

All missionaries face stress and even trauma as they move through the life-changing consequences of their first term overseas. This couple, having made what seemed a simple response to a call of God, find themselves increasingly fearful as the wheels of administrative machinery moved them relentlessly forward to a future of overwhelming uncertainty. They want to say 'stop,' but don't know how to until a hidden pressure erupts in London. Justified sympathy and understanding leads to the repatriation of this fine young couple to their home territory, and to lessons we all learn from this experience.

~~~ ~~~ ~~~

The varied matters which come to the Chief's business table include proposals for new allowance scales. Here we tend to support the Chief's approval if the increase desired is modest and in line with a country's cost of living increase.

I feel uneasy about this procedure, however, recognizing that the area of the world I represent is unfairly behind other missionary territories on a comparative basis. But how to prove this? Fortunately, after some research, I contact an agency that helps multi-national companies with this same problem. For every dollar paid to an employee in the U.K., they will tell his company how much that employee needs to be paid to live on the same scale in Hong Kong or Havana, Delhi or Detroit, or anywhere else in the world. And they produce constantly updated figures for differing lifestyles.

The report I present to the Chief of the Staff at a business meeting is studied with appreciated care, and proves my point. It cannot be implemented fully at that time, however, due to the great strain it would put on international funding. The territories of South Asia are among those not self-supporting.

~~~ ~~~ ~~~

The General's business meetings, held in her office, deal with major items relating to policy, appointments, difficulties and discipline. The General always makes sure that everyone present gives an opinion, and that action follows any decision made. Special consideration is shown for areas of the world politically isolated or facing exceptional strife, disturbance or restriction.

Burma (known as Myanmar) highlights this. General Burrows instructs me to visit Burma soon after my taking office to commission the first training session in many years. She also asks me to raise Burma's status from a region under the oversight of the North-Eastern India Territory (as it was then) to a Command under the leadership of its own senior officer, Lieut.-Colonel Saratha Peiriswami.

All missionary officers had been compelled to leave Burma 20 years earlier. Through the intervening years of almost total isolation, Lt.-Col. Peiriswami, with great courage and unwavering determination, maintained the Army's presence, spirit and witness. What a privilege to meet her in Rangoon (now Yangon), to observe her frugal lifestyle and share the austere but joyous atmosphere of Salvation Army fellowship in that city.

Neither can I forget a journey up-country over rough roads to Pyu as a rare visitor to the well-run children's home where the young folk proudly dance and sing for their international visitor. At the nearby corps I feel like the Apostle Paul visiting an isolated Christian community on one of his missionary journeys. The hunger for teaching and fellowship, and the reluctance to say goodbye mellow my heart.

More moving moments follow enroute back to Yangon as we pause at the immaculately-kept Taukkyan Cemetery which honours the memory of tens of thousands of allied servicemen who died in south-east Asia in the Second World War.

Restrictions reimposed on travel into Myanmar prevents the Indian leader whose territory partially borders on this neighbouring country from making further supportive visits. Always ready for a flexibility of action that produced positive results, the General agrees on oversight from Sri Lanka; and for some time a missionary officer successfully obtains visas for periodic instructional seminars.

This support proves vital when illness compels the ageing and frail Colonel Peiriswami to retire shortly after her anticipated successor resigns. Problems compound when the second choice for leadership, a young officer fluent in English who had attended the International College for Officers in London dies suddenly while visiting in a remote area of Northern Myanmar.

Recently it has been found that Singaporean officers can obtain entry into Myanmar more easily than from other nearby areas. The General has therefore made an appropriate adjustment of oversight responsibility from the I.S. for South Asia to the I.S. for the South Pacific and East Asia.

In our fragmented and politically disturbed world today, this is one small illustration of the constant response a General has to make to unexpected problems of ever-changing variety and complexity.

## Dealing with Distresses

At International Headquarters we always try to be pro-active rather than re-active. Long range planning is an accepted principle of good management. Financial budgeting and human resource planning are vital to effective administration. Matching limited resources of money and personnel to unlimited needs and opportunities present a constant challenge to a Movement whose ministry reaches more than 100 countries.

Replacement of missionaries returning to homelands is an ever-pressing demand, as well as top leadership changes. The General and the Chief of the Staff require international secretaries constantly to up-date their long-range leadership strategies; and the same is expected of territorial commanders within their own responsibilities.

But the best laid plans can go awry! Cherished hopes can be dashed. Unexpected events take place, situations arise or circumstances develop that cannot be controlled. And they dramatically affect the lives and service of all, God's people not excepted. Often such situations create extreme distress, and painful repercussions ensue at I.H.Q.

I am awakened in the middle of one night by our home phone ringing. It is 3:00 a.m. A distraught territorial commander 6,000 miles away gives me the sad news that his missionary chief secretary, Lieut.-Colonel Railton Williams, has died—suddenly and unexpectedly. Railton, injured in a road accident ten days earlier had been expected to recover. The privileged but sad duty is mine to conduct a memorial service at I.H.Q. for this personal friend who, with his wife Joan, had shared the India road with us for many years.

Other repercussions need immediate attention. Not least, of course, the unexpected and urgent need to choose a successor. The General's special gift of remembering capable officers around the world enables her to make suitable decisions when no obvious choice can be recommended. Necessarily, though, senior appointment changes involve chain reactions and a number of senior officer appointment changes will frequently follow.

Unpredictable, too, are the crisis situations that arise, particularly in developing countries. They can scar for life those involved, and bring consternation and anxiety to their associates, as well as worry and concern to I.H.Q.

Such a case arises when a phone call comes to me from halfway round the world intimating that a group of officers travelling to a militant-controlled area of a South Asian country were attacked by a rebel group. Two were separated from the others and almost killed, and all subjected to the most harrowing 24-hours of their lives. Two officers—including a missionary—have to be hospitalized with suspected heart attacks.

As my wife and I are about to visit South Asia, we adjust our itinerary so that we can visit the territory concerned and see what effect the frightening incident has on those involved.

In asking the officers to share their experience with me, I apologize for the necessity of reviving a dreadful encounter. I explain that we at I.H.Q. want to know a little more clearly what happened, and what its long-term effects might be upon them. This can help us advise others how to respond in similar emergency situations. We also offer counselling.

The Territorial Headquarters' van is proceeding to an institution where a difficult situation has arisen. The national territorial commander and his wife had travelled the same road a week earlier attempting to resolve the problem. Now six T.H.Q.

officers, three of one racial origin, two of another, and a missionary, are on a follow-up mission.

As they cross the final I.P.K.F. (International Peacekeeping Force) checkpoint before entering the less secure area of "militant" (some prefer "terrorist") activity, they are told that there has been a little incident earlier, but all is well to travel on. A short distance down the road, however, a group of militant young men halt them. They are heavily armed, angry, and argumentative. They threaten to set the vehicle and occupants on fire. On discovering that two of the passengers belonged to the dominant race whose government they are fighting, the terrorists become even more agitated and aggressive.

The two officers are knocked around with weapons and pushed into roadside rooms. At gunpoint, the remainder of the party are forced out of their vehicle as well. Before being put on a halted bus they are threatened with death if they tell anyone of the incident or leave the bus before it reaches its ultimate destination. In spite of a threat not to get off the bus, the four remaining officers do so at the next military base eight or nine kilometres down the road. Here they plead desperately for the government forces to rescue their friends.

Meanwhile, the two hijacked officers are taken into a room and beaten severely. Both are given divine strength and there are neither cries nor tears. The married officer commits his wife and children, and his own spirit, to God, believing the end is near. This conviction is heightened when, taken outside briefly, they discover that the van and their friends have gone. The two terrified officers are then separated, and the male officer is taken to a room where there are many weapons, more people, and a rope hanging from a roof beam.

After his shoes had been removed, the Salvation Army captain is hung from the roof by crossed hands with only his toes touching the floor. The group leader explains that this is retaliation for 17 of his people who have just been killed by government troops. In the interrogation that follows, the captain is asked a few questions and then battered everywhere before the questioning continues. This continued 50 or 60 times.

Meanwhile, the I.P.K.F. officer at the forward United Nations camp is under relentless pressure to phone his counterpart at the more southerly checkpoint. The Salvationists, who included a Westerner, plead for urgent intervention on behalf of their two hijacked associates.

The story is too lengthy to continue in detail, but all agree a miracle occurs when the two captive officers are released by I.P.K.F. intervention—the woman officer having been treated even more cruelly than the man—and join their friends amid tears of overwhelming relief and rejoicing. After another day and some further harrowing journeying, the van and its exhausted passengers arrived home again.

Because I.P.K.F. officials have advised not to discuss the incident, rumours spread that tend to generate disharmony among the territory's racially divided Salvationists. This requires careful and wise handling. Several of those involved need time to recover, one is hospitalized and the missionary officer is advised to take an early homeland furlough.

What an inspiration to talk to the two officers primarily involved! In being tested to the point of death itself, they discover that their faith can stand up to the worst that life can hold for them. God, they affirm, is totally reliable and sufficient. I am humbled to hear their genuine testimony of strength granted to them, and their gratitude to God for the miracle of life spared.

It is encouraging to know that in South Asia, and around the world, we have officers whose spiritual integrity and maturity is powerfully confirmed when tested to the limit. We who live in lands of greater stability and security must never forget the uncertainty and peril faced by national and missionary co-workers in other lands.

### An Army of Disciplined Flexibility

The General is clearly upset. I am in Trivandrum, Southern India, and the Army's international leader is phoning me from London. "Your under-secretary here tells me that you had a rough day yesterday. I understand that the six senior officers to whom you conveyed disciplinary decisions approved by me before you left London reacted by causing a great commotion and refusing to leave territorial headquarters. Tell me again what happened after that."

"Well, General, not only did they refuse to leave the building, but they also had about 60 supporters at the gate who would not allow anyone to leave the compound. I was, in fact, 'gharoed' (confined to the building) with other officers for eight hours." Some fruitless discussions with much shouting took place during this period. (Meanwhile, the territorial commander, with Rahab-like circumvention, managed to get a note out of his upstairs office window at the back of the building requesting a little food be brought to us by the same means.)

"By evening it was felt necessary to call the police to clear the building and allow our safe exit. Forty Salvationists or supporters were temporarily placed in police custody and then released under promise of good behaviour. The territorial commander has received some threats, and the police advise us not to conduct public events."

"And what do you suggest should be done now, Commissioner?" asks General Eva Burrows. I am making an extensive last tour of India prior to retirement, and am keen to deal with the escalating problems in this one territory. Administratively,

India has five other Salvation Army 'territories.' This particular troubled territory has about 600 officers (ministers), 300 corps (churches) and societies (operated from corps), 16 schools and 26 institutions.

Briefly I respond to the General's question. "In spite of assurances from the suspended officers that they will immediately stop all disturbances in the territory if the proposed disciplinary measures are withdrawn, I do not feel that we can retract on the reasonable steps already taken, and decisions made. Nor do I feel, even now, that we should dismiss these recalcitrant officers. The commission appointed to look into the problems here on your behalf arrives in Bombay in a couple of days, and I will adjust my itinerary so that I can meet them and bring them up to date on the situation. They may need extra freedom of action."

"That's no problem. Keep in touch with me, and in the meantime I hope the remainder of your tour is a little more enjoyable."

Personally, it is a great disappointment for Eva and me to have our farewell tour cancelled. I had visited this vibrant territory many times over the previous two decades and had always received the most gracious hospitality and friendly cooperation. Heart-warming memories remain.

This is our last tour of South Asia, and there are many highlight experiences. Nineteen flights, interspersed with train and car journeys, take us from strife-torn Punjab to strife-torn Sri Lanka, from the sub-Himalayan hills of Darjeeling to the Blue Mountains of southern India. From Karachi to Calcutta, Dhaka to Delhi, Mizoram to Madras, and much more.

There are conferences to chair; schools, hospitals, clinics and many other institutions to visit; meetings to conduct at corps and territorial and divisional centres; and our own farewell gatherings to enjoy and remember. We look back over more than

20 years of service linked to South Asia and thank God for it, and for the lovely people who have enriched our lives.

The one incident just described only highlights the fact that Salvation Army administration, in any global setting, is far more complex than could have been imagined in the pioneer days of Booth-Tucker and his missionary vanguard more than 120 years ago.

How much more so at the international level, where it is so necessary to maintain unity of purpose and principle, yet allow for justified flexibility. That flexibility must recognize the variances of culture and tradition, as well as political and religious environment, within the many countries in which the Army fulfils its mission.

The India incident illustrates the point. In South Asian cultures generally, dharnas (picketing), bandhs (shut downs) and gharoing (confinement) are usually considered acceptable means of protest. Also, the importance of saving face must be understood when disciplining senior officers. Further, (and especially in South India), caste consciousness and pride can be significant factors. So can insensitivity and lack of effective communication on the part of a territory's leadership.

I have always been an admirer of the late General Frederick Coutts, and particularly of his writings. He had the gift of using words with clarity, conciseness and cogency. Some words from an address given to officers, and reprinted in his book *Essentials of Christian Experience*, have been helpful to me in my role as an international secretary. The Scripture text is, "We are troubled on every side, yet not distressed; we are perplexed, but not in despair." (2 Corinthians 4:8)

In his comments General Coutts made some humorous remarks about having been "reared in the now obsolete dogma of the infallibility of Salvation Army leadership, at any rate from the level of divisional commander upward!" He then went on: "None of us is infallible, not even the youngest of us. And the more that hinges upon a decision, the greater our perplexity can be." He then quotes the response of a predecessor, General Wilfred Kitching, to a question regarding the most satisfying experience of retirement: "The freedom from the responsibility of making decisions affecting the well-being of other people."

How then can we make any final decisions at all? Again, General Coutts has the right word: "Never self-confidently, much less ever carelessly or casually. Off-the-cuff judgements, snap decisions, have no place in the affairs of the Kingdom."

Certainly this was my experience at I.H.Q. as I worked with the General, the Chief of the Staff, associate international secretaries and departmental staff.

## *REFLECTIONS*

Decisions are not personal but relate to leadership responsibilities. They are of infinite variety, sometimes consultative, and invariably affecting the well-being of others. Those who judge shall also be judged. How necessary that we continually search our own hearts, hunger and thirst after integrity, and seek better to know and emulate the mind of Christ.

## CHAPTER 8: 1991 - 2000

## A DECADE OF CONSEQUENCES

### *Blessings Beyond our Deserving*

"Everybody, soon or late, sits down to a banquet of consequences." Robert Louis Stevenson's rather startling statement has significant relevance as this memoir now reviews our first nine years of retirement and last decade of the twentieth century.

The choices, commitments, and some would say, sacrifices made in earlier years seem to bring consequences of immeasurable joy and blessings beyond our deserving. The most significant consequences are, of course, the memories that this book has sought to revive. To journey through retirement with such a banquet of memories is a priceless treasure.

We cannot say we longed for retirement. Nor can we say we feared it. It was not the end of the journey, but a change of course; not a full stop but a punctuation mark. What about an exclamation mark? Writers are taught to use exclamation marks sparingly, but surely retirement is an appropriate occasion.

After all, it is no ordinary transition that finds one rushing through some final business in the General's office five minutes before driving out of International Headquarters one day, and the next morning waking up to the reality that there would be no journey to London, no phone calls, no business meetings. One is no longer participating in significant decisions. Life at I.H.Q. is moving on serenely and efficiently without you. Ah, Shakespeare, you are right. All the world's a stage and we all have our entrances and exits. A good dose of humility is our best elixir.

## Return to Canada

Actually, April 1, 1991 finds Evangeline and me in Paris where good friends help us memorably to mark the first day of retirement. Still fresh in our minds, of course, is our official retirement ceremony at International Headquarters conducted by General Eva Burrows, as well as several other celebrations that all too generously recognize our service as Salvation Army officers. But now it's time to look ahead to a significant change of location as well as activity. Canada is on our horizon.

An eagerly anticipated moment arrives when, on arrival at Toronto Pearson Airport, we are enthusiastically greeted by family members and taken to our temporary home in Oakville. No longer thousands of miles to separate us. No longer all too infrequent family reunions. No longer packing suitcases and completing visa documentation. We can live within half-an-hour's drive of all our three children.

Initial days are fully occupied making accommodation and furnishing decisions, and becoming familiar with retirement allowance arrangements in relation to the Canadian dollar's purchasing power. We joyfully participate in our youngest son's wedding and, over the course of the next few years, share in welcoming the arrival of six of our eight grandchildren. Few experiences can be more pleasurable than sharing in family celebrations, and watching one granddaughter and seven grandsons moving from fragile babyhood toward, and into, maturing teenagers. And what a privilege for Eva and me to know that in these later years of life we are encompassed by the ever-watchful care and love of Heather and Mike, Howard and Cheryl and Graham and Julie.

Few retirees are ready after a busy and active working life to settle overnight for a rocking chair lifestyle. A transition period of diminishing responsibilities and gradually increasing leisure time is necessary before retirement is fully embraced. Eva and I happily accept the offer of part-time roles within The Salvation Army; myself returning to the Editorial Department in Oakville, and Eva joining the staff at Toronto Grace Hospital, a palliative and chronic care facility.

### The 'Write' Role for Me

For me, it is great to return to the editorial department where many lasting friendships are renewed, and to writing tasks for which I have always felt a natural and developed ability. It is somewhat of a disappointment that after four happy years the Oakville office is closed and its staff transferred to the newly-purchased territorial headquarters building in Toronto. For me this will mean a minimum of three hours of round-trip journeying each day—not a desirable retirement activity! It is time to look at options.

Attendance at several Christian writers' conferences increasingly makes me aware of a need for writers who are Christian to reach out to a secular press generally oblivious to, or dismissive of, religious values and perspectives. I have a compelling urge to consider this new avenue of mission challenge.

Eva and I are now living in Burlington and I am successful in making friendly contacts with the local office of *'The Spectator'* where a twice-weekly insert of local news is produced. The friendly editor gives me both opportunities for publication and advice on newspaper style, practices and expectations. After a couple of years there is a significant change. The Burlington office is closed and local news integrated into the parent paper, now renamed *'The Hamilton Spectator.'* The paper's outreach is widened to cover the entire Niagara Peninsular and the western end of Lake Ontario.

To make inroads into the large newsroom at Hamilton is more difficult, and I am advised that they are not short of freelance writers. However, opportunity is given to apply for a position on the Community Editorial Board that will allow me, if accepted, to write a 1200 word article every six weeks for a period of 18-24 months. There is no pay, but a guarantee of publication with no restrictions on subject matter, and opportunities for periodic discussions with the editor-in-chief and senior staff.

My application is followed by an interview and acceptance. What writer does not feel considerable satisfaction and pride when a three-column article appears on the editorial page with the author's name and accompanying photo? The painful process of converting a bright idea into an article worthy of publication is suddenly justified.

The subjects I choose range from a serious consideration of the question, 'Can war ever be justified?' to light-hearted comments on my contacts with the British royal family. Looking back over more than twenty articles published, I found myself primarily writing on themes of peace, forgiveness, war experiences and purposeful living; always overtly or directly elevating Christian standards and values.

### *Community Involvements*

During this writing period, I widen my community contacts and activities. Eva and I love the Army that has given us opportunities—and now memories—always to be cherished. But there is a world beyond the Army's diversified outreach that desperately needs Christian witnesses who make faith intelligible, desirable and attainable. We want to be part of such a wider ministry also.

Thus it is that I volunteer—and am accepted after interview—as a member of the City of Burlington's Heritage Committee. As citizens of a comparatively young country we Canadians, generally, do not fully appreciate the desirability of preserving our cultural and built heritage. Europe and Asia have much to teach us. We need to safeguard and value buildings and artifacts that link us to our past and that will increasingly provide the security of roots and values so necessary in our rapidly changing society.

During six years with the committee (including consecutive years as vice chair, chair and past chair) it is a privilege to work with dedicated citizens and a generally supportive city council to protect heritage properties from over-zealous developers, constantly update our archival records and continue to enhance public awareness that massive city expansion must happily blend old and new.

One of the joys of retirement is the freedom to switch from one activity to another whenever whim or preference dictates. We are no longer making destiny-shaping decisions! A newspaper advertisement alerted Eva and me to the opportunities of voluntary service with the Victorian Order of Nurses (VON) particularly in the area of supporting palliative care patients who choose to remain at home.

My most vivid memory is of giving a few hours a week to the supportive care of Ray, a recently retired gentleman with Lou Gehrig's disease (ALS). To share the last six months of Ray's desperate struggle to overcome diminishing independence as his body systematically shuts down is emotionally draining, but a valuable learning experience.

It is also a fulfilling one-year experience to set up the chaplaincy program at a long-term care centre in Oakville. Other activities include speaking at civic and school Remembrance Day services, a variety of Christian ministry responsibilities at our Burlington Salvation Army corps and, by email, editing copy for the English edition of the national *'War Cry'* for India.

## Recreational Pleasures

In the area of relaxation, sailing is my most exhilarating and invigorating activity. It begins soon after retirement when the proximity of our apartment to Oakville harbour on Lake Ontario awakens my nautical instincts.

For two years I enroll in winter night-school sailing classes. Then starts my adventure as a spare crew member at the local yacht club, and learning the intricacies of yacht racing. On one particular boat the woman skipper teaches me the highly competitive nature of yacht racing. She is an excellent skipper, but does not suffer fools gladly. I sometimes find it difficult to meet her expectations.

After our move to Burlington I join the nearby Bronte Yacht Club, but there seems less frequent need for replacement crew. A thoughtful skipper suggests I might speak to the race chairman whose committee boat manages the bi-weekly races. He is often short of crew. After taking more courses I become a valued member of this august body, and quickly discovered that the oversight of highly-competitive yacht races is a precise and demanding task—but great fun!

Vivid to memory are evenings of sheer delight as the beauty of a sun setting on gently rippling water surrounds one with a sense of tranquility rarely experienced in the hurly-burly of everyday life. These are moments of breathtaking serenity.

But competitive yachtsmen much prefer a stiff wind and boisterous waters to test their sailing abilities. One night an unexpected change of weather requires us hurriedly to hoist the 'abandon race' flag. Quickly a black and stormy night is upon us; it is no pleasant task to search for missing boats. At an unusually late hour all the yachts are accounted for and safe in or near harbour. All, that is, except one catamaran that capsized and no efforts by the two crew members or ourselves were able to right it. Difficult too, is the task of securing a couple of lines on the waterlogged boat and towing it, and its crew, slowly to the nearest beach in pitch darkness. It is a storm-soaked, somewhat exhausted but relieved race committee crew who finally dock within the protecting and welcoming arms of Bronte Harbour just before midnight.

How symbolic sailing is of the journey of life! One day calm and serene, the next boisterously challenging, or even distressingly precarious. My association with sailing continues for most of the decade.

Cycling is another appealing recreational exercise, and between May and December I usually cycle three or four times a week and total 500 - 1,200 kilometres. I enjoy cycling even more than walking now, but must admit I have a secret routine. Halfway around my circular route I pause for a breakfast coffee and English muffin, and a glance at the newspaper! The pause that refreshes.

What grand family times we share together, too! Numerous birthday parties and other occasions of celebration, camping, watching grandchildren develop in sporting activities and academic success, school graduations and special activities, all are a constant pleasure and joy.

The record of this period, though, would not be complete without some reference to natural aging problems that increase with advancing years.

I am 70 before taking my first prescribed medications regularly. Since then visits to doctors' offices, laboratory tests, and even hospital emergency departments have become a not unnatural part of life. Eva has had knee replacement surgery, and both of us have spent short periods in hospital and learned to adjust to the intriguing world of medical care.

However, as we reach the end of the 20$^{th}$ century we are keeping remarkably well, and ever grateful to God for basic good health and countless mercies.

As a new century dawns we enjoy the most thrilling experience of retirement years—an eastern Mediterranean cruise which takes us to historic and biblically significant ports in Greece, Turkey, Egypt and Italy, followed by two glorious weeks visiting family and friends in England. We also share a delightful reunion gathering in London with 30 former India missionary associates, arranged by friends of many years, Commissioners David and Vera Durman.

### *Time to Look Back*

So the 20$^{th}$ Century passes into history, and these recollections describing a unique journey must take a gigantic leap backwards 100 years. These reminiscences intentionally began by examining the thoughts of a young war-veteran, still in his early twenties. He was clearly restless and we noted the pivotal choices and decisions of succeeding years that stilled the storm of restlessness, and brought a banquet of peace and fulfillment to retirement years. But we still haven't answered a key question. What led to the restlessness? Had the environment and lifestyle of earlier years made deep, irresistible impressions on heart and mind that needed resolution now in choices more significant than any made before? For our answer we need to journey back not only to earliest years, but also to the year 1900, so that we can note the influence of culture, heritage and family life on this maturing young man.

Renowned philosophers such as Soren Kierkegaard have said that while life must be lived forward, it must be understood backward. In essence, the then General Frederick Coutts said the same thing in a great 1965 centenary congress gathering. The General spoke on the text "Look to the rock from which you are cut..." He urged his listeners to remember their heritage, not only as Salvationists but through Scriptural history. "God by his Spirit," he summed up, "is saying to us through this ancient word: look at what I have done. And then, look at what you should do. What he would have you do, do quickly."

## *REFLECTIONS*

Freedom! Freedom again to choose where we will live and what we will do.

Not a freedom to forget our covenant and calling, though. We are still ordained ministers of the Gospel, and as opportunities arise fulfill a continuing mission. We are to reflect every day by our actions more than our words, perhaps, a faith that is persuasively desirable and achievable.

And retirement, too, is a time to reflect on the maze of life, and the serendipitous consequences of many lifetime choices and decisions in which we have sought the mind of Christ.

## Chapter 9: 1900 - 1935

## A Goodly Heritage

### *A New Century Dawns*

We turn back the pages of this life story, then, to the beginning of the 20$^{th}$ century, where I find my roots, and examine briefly the environment and culture of my birth.

As the year 1900 dawned, few could have predicted that the new century would bring: two world wars, the atom bomb, travel to the moon, international terrorism, unimagined global communications, the rise and fall of communism, and a Western culture which set aside traditional ethical and religious values for a lifestyle that largely worships science, technology and hedonistic sexuality.

During the last decade of the 1800s and the first decade of the 1900s, Great Britain was busy looking after her vast empire and interests. Militarily she was constantly involved in wars, occupations, bombardments and protective activities. Highlighting these were Kitchener's defeat of the Sudanese dervishes at the Battle of Omdurman, and the Boer War in which General Charles Gordon was defeated and killed at the siege of Mafeking.

In other parts of the world, war breaks out between Italy and Abyssinia, and the Sino-Chinese war ends; the United States and Spain fight over Cuba, the Boxer Rebellion causes upheaval in China, and Japan and Russia declare war. No wonder The Salvation Army feels comfortable with its marching bands and quasi-military structure. No wonder 'Onward Christian soldiers' becomes a favourite song of Salvationists!

It is also a time of inventiveness and industrial development. The Eiffel Tower becomes a stunning landmark in Paris, and a 10-storey 'skyscraper' rises in St. Louis, U.S.A. Karl Benz builds his first four-wheel car, and Henry Ford institutes the assembly line production of his Model T. The Wright Brothers fly Kitty Hawk for 59 seconds, and Louis Bleriot is the first flyer to cross the English Channel. Marconi invents wireless telegraphy and Count von Zeppelin his airship, while Marie Currie discovers radium, and Aspirin is first marketed.

At the beginning of the century, prominent names in the arts, science and culture include Rudyard Kipling, Peter Tchaikovsky, Edgar Elgar, John Philip Sousa, Sigmund Freud, Albert Einstein, Arthur Conan Doyle and Vladimir Lenin.

For The Salvation Army also, the years just prior to, and immediately following 1900 see dramatic change and progress— though not without its street processions, outdoor meetings and halls being attacked by mobs, often violently. In one year alone 669 Salvationists (251 of them women) are injured and 56 Army buildings damaged. The Founder's motto, 'Go for sinners and go for the worst,' does not sit well with brewers and others whose livelihoods are affected by the Army's boisterous evangelism.

In the days before television, cell phones and our present society's multi-faceted distractions, public houses were a worker's haven between the dreary workplace and a cramped little industrial area dwelling. But public houses were also the cause of widespread drunkenness and hungry families.

Nevertheless, the Army's exuberant style of worship and witness meet with astonishing success. In the summer of 1899, for instance, the Army in Britain records 2,765 corps and 8,639 officers. Six months later these numbers have increased to 2,828 corps and 9,921 officers.

Alongside this remarkable ability to bring all sorts and conditions of men and women into dramatic life changing relationship with a living Christ, is the parallel expansion of the Army's soup and salvation brand of evangelism outside the British Isles. By the turn of the century, this lively branch of the Christian Church with its uniforms, bands, tambourines, outdoor witness and fiery 'common peoples' gospel message, coupled with its selfless ministry to the poorest of the poor, has established itself in 35 countries.

### *Shy Young Man – Winsome Lass*

It is into this world and environment that we now comment on significant aspects of my heritage. In the year 1900 Bramwell Coles, my father, is the young 13-year-old son of Salvation Army corps officers, Captain and Mrs. Albert Coles. Mother was a six-year-old daughter of Captain and Mrs. Edwin LeButt. (Personally, I never knew my maternal grandparents, and hardly knew my paternal grandfather.)

My father's birth certificate shows that he is born to 'Albert and Maria Coles—Captains in The Salvation Army—on February 22, 1887 in Cambridge, England.' I also possess a copy of an undertaker's notice that Marie Coles died on April 20, 1893 at age 32 years. She is buried in Forest Hill Cemetery, London. Father has four sisters, Gertrude, Florence, Mildred and Maria, and they are all left motherless at very young ages. Almost 18 months later, Grandfather Coles marries again, this time to a strict and stern former school governess named Emely Kearsley. Regrettably it seems she does not bond well with the children, certainly not to my sensitive father who always treasures the memory of his birth mother with special love and affection.

Father welcomes the new century by deliberately deciding to give his heart and life over to God at the 1899 New Year's Eve 'watch night' meeting conducted by his father. "I definitely gave my heart to God that night," he later recalled. Little could this shy and reserved boy imagine where his commitment would lead in the ensuing days and the impact his developing musical talents would have on the Army in the years ahead.

In 1904, Father moves with his parents to Chalk Farm Corps in London, a move which author Wally Court says in a recent illuminating Bramwell Coles biography 'had a monumental effect in determining the future direction of his life.' By that time, the Salvation Army has 20,000 Salvationists playing and singing in over 1,000 bands and songster brigades (choirs) in Great Britain.

In the forefront of excellence is the Chalk Farm (London) Band under its renowned bandmaster, Alfred W. Punchard. He is a mentor par excellence, and father's life begins to blossom. Almost overnight the young Bramwell Coles becomes a Salvationist celebrity by earning a third prize in band music competitions in 1907 and 1908. These are festival programs of great appeal and held at the Army's spacious Clapton Congress Hall, in London.

In 1909, 4,000 people again crowd into the Army's largest meeting place for the annual music festival program. Chalk Farm Band is on stage with six other bands and two songster brigades. Again there are moments of mounting anticipation as the third and second prize winners are announced. Then the International Staff Band plays the first prize-winning march (later renamed the Chalk Farm March)—and father is named as the composer. He is 22 years of age. Hesitantly he stands to acknowledge the applause and recognition. What an exciting and long-to-be-remembered day for this reserved young man!

When his parents transfer to another corps appointment, father chooses to remain behind in 'digs' at Chalk Farm. He works as an office boy at the Army's international headquarters in London, and then takes a shorthand clerk's job at a solicitor's office just off the Strand. Meanwhile with all-consuming passion he studies harmony and develops natural skills in composing music suitable for Salvation Army use.

Father enters International Training College in 1914 and is commissioned a captain to North Ormsby Corps, Middlesborough, and the next year transferred to New Barnet Corps. It may well be during his brief stay at New Barnet that he first meets his wife to be—a young Salvationist at neighbouring High Barnet Corps—named Agnes LeButt. (I have been interested to read in Wally Court's biography *In the Firing Line*, however, that they first met five years earlier when father was given the mission of delivering a letter from international headquarters to the Army's insurance society offices nearby, where 17 year-old Agnes worked).

How and when Agnes LeButt's parents meet and join The Salvation Army I do not know. A photograph taken in 1908 shows Brigadier Edward LeButt sitting beside Bramwell Booth. (In 1880, at the age of 24, Bramwell had become Chief of the Staff and remained in this role for the next 32 years until taking over the Generalship on the death of his father.) LeButt is identified as private secretary to the Chief of the Staff.

Also surviving the passage of years is a letter written by the Founder himself in his strong, bold but hurried handwriting, and dated August 11, 1910:

> "*My dear LeButt:*
>
> *I am sorry to learn that you have been so poorly these last few days. I thought you were not well on Monday, and I was terribly run down myself so could not get my thoughts into proper understandable language. However, I trust you are*

*improved and improving as I certainly through mercy am myself.*

*"These are days for the exercise of faith by all of us, and specially those of us who are at the heart of things. Remember me to your suffering wife. I pray that God may uphold and comfort and heal her. The Chief looks better for his few days respite and change.*

*"In faith and hope and love, believe me.*

*Yours in the blood and fire. As ever.*

*William Booth."*

'Blood and fire' is a Salvation Army theological shorthand for the saving grace of Jesus made efficacious through his shed blood on the Cross, and the purifying presence of the Holy Spirit (fire) in the life of the believer.

Another piece of memorabilia is a four page article printed in the April 1916 edition of *All the World*, an Army magazine that emphasized global perspectives. Written by Mrs. Brigadier Carpenter (whose husband later became General), the article begins with the announcement, "Promoted to Glory"—the Army's term for passing away—"Mrs. Lieut.-Colonel Le Butt, nee Charlotte Smiles, who came out of Folkestone in March 1891. From High Barnet on December 27, 1915."

The writer explains that her sketch "intends to suggest a few features in a life which, though strangely hidden from public gaze and bound by affliction's bond, manifested the graces of the Holy Spirit in a way that made many adore the grace of God." What was 'afflictions bond'? The author explains:

"Some 18 years ago, Mrs. LeButt was caught in a heavy downpour of rain which resulted in the beginning of attacks of rheumatism. This illness steadily increased, and six years ago a complete collapse of her physical strength left her a helpless invalid. How great a calamity was this to a home where there were six children—the eldest 16 and the youngest two—mothers will particularly appreciate."

Paragraph after paragraph of lavish eulogy follow. A few sentences have particular relevance. "Perhaps her most prized possession was a tender letter written to her by the dear old General (William Booth) with his own hand a few days before his last operation. Then it was apparently a crowning joy to her when, a few months before her death, her eldest child, Cadet Agnes (my mother) entered the Salvation Army training college. And how keen she was to offer my mother a little advice:

"'The world is longing for love and peace, Agnes,' she would say. 'Scatter these blessings wherever you go. Everyone can do that. And oh, remember your influence! Be careful that all your actions and words are worthy of a true Salvation Army officer. I have prayed this for you.'"

### *A Marriage Made in Heaven*

Now comes a happy day when Lieutenant Agnes LeButt and Captain Bramwell Coles are married in the Army's famous Regent Hall on Oxford Street in London. Commissioner George Mitchell conducts the wedding on August 9, 1917. Father chose his life partner carefully. Many years later I remember him saying that he had always wanted his children to have the kind of home life he had never enjoyed. He certainly couldn't have given us a more wonderful mother.

The first few years of marriage see many changes for the young couple. No sooner have they settled into the leadership of the Hendon Corps than father is required to enlist in His Majesty's Services—the Royal Army Pay Corps. But again, no sooner has he joined the military for the last months of World War I than he is hospitalized with malaria. A consequent early discharge follows.

During this period he writes two of his most remembered marches, "Under Two Flags" and "In the Firing Line," as well as the epic meditation "Man of Sorrows." A few years later this latter piece is performed at a great festival in London honoured by the presence of the future King George VI and Queen Elizabeth.

Further changes come for my parents when father is appointed to the editorial department of international headquarters and spends many weeks away from home reporting the campaigns conducted by General Bramwell Booth and Mrs. Booth throughout the British Isles and on the Continent. Then in 1923, father transfers to the music editorial department due to the temporary health breakdown of its music editor.

Concurrently with these appointments he takes on the roles of songster leader at East Finchley Corps and then band instructor at Wood Green, as well as being a guest participant in the tours of the Chalk Farm Band. Music continued to flow unabated from his pen. And not only stirring marches. Now Salvationists are being inspired by his sensitive meditations and selections—"Atonement," "Pilgrimage" and "Discipleship" being among that number.

In mid-1925 a stunning location change is given to Adjutant and Mrs. Bramwell Coles. Now the parents of four children whose ages ranged from six months to six years, they are appointed to the territorial headquarters editorial department in Toronto, Canada.

The next ten years proved a very happy period for the family. Three Canadian sons are added to the family—of whom I am one—and deep bonds develop that in later years result in most of the family returning to Canada to establish their homes.

Father's writing enlivened the Salvation Army flagship paper, *The War Cry*, and broadened the horizon of its Salvationist musician readers. His presence also brought a new dimension to the Army music scene in Canada and the Unites States. To quote

Wally Court's biography once again, "With over 50 bands and songster brigades operating within 250 miles from Toronto, 'Meet Coles' programs became a popular weekend feature."

A highlight visit to the U.S.A. takes place in 1930 when Golden Jubilee celebrations are held in New York. Father shares superlative music events with such household names in American—and world-wide—brass band circles as Edwin Franko Goldman and John Philip Sousa.

Mother could not accompany father for many of these events. Understandably, the care of seven young children took more hours than there were to each day. But she went about the endless routines of washing, sewing, ironing and meal preparation with unfailing cheerfulness and winsome temperament.

Father often had duties with various Toronto bands, including Dovercourt, Earlscourt and Toronto Temple, and Sunday evenings we younger children would stay at home. Mother would gather us around the piano for a sing-song. We all had our favourite choruses. One brother liked to choose, 'The devil and me we can't agree, glory hallelujah…;' another 'I will make you fishers of men…' My favourite, apparently, was 'God save the king!'.

Father did find time, though, to make sure we all helped mother in every way we could. Ours was an ordered and happy home. Quite often, too, Father would want to do some composing, and he would call mother into the living room to critique some ideas he had, though his mastery of the piano was somewhat limited. I remember him listening to an orchestral record of Tchaikovsky's music and replaying again and again a difficult part he wished to transcribe for brass bands. How difficult to bring within the limited instrumentation of a brass band the full beauty of classical music played by great orchestras. And how difficult for we children to keep as quiet as we are asked to be!

We live on Davisville Avenue near Mount Pleasant, and edging a park. The Salvation Army owns a number of homes on this street that Salvationists and neighbours called 'holy row.' Some of these homes, including our own, are later demolished to extend the park. We younger Coles boys attend Davisville School, just east of Mount Pleasant. I still remember marching into our classrooms to the stirring sound of Sousa marches played over the loudspeaker system. Another recollection is of fainting in the school yard while standing to attention for some ceremonial event.

There is only one other significant memory. As I am walking home from school one day a brother runs up to me with some unbelievably exciting news. We are moving to England!

## *REFLECTIONS*

Having followed the successive consequences of life choices and decisions, this autobiographer is now looking at his roots and heritage.

What part did they play in shaping the choices that are now the history of a life?

There is no doubt that my Salvation Army roots go back to the Movement's beginnings. Nor can there be any doubt that godly parents instilled strong Christian values and character into my young heart.

As the chapter concludes, I still have to go through years of discovering life's wider horizons: who I am, and life's ultimate meaning and purpose for me.

## CHAPTER 10: 1935 - 1946

## A TEENAGER IN MOMENTOUS DAYS

### *Early Excitement and Adventure*

Yes, as I amble home from my Toronto school one winter day, late in 1935, a brother runs to me with startling news. "Dud, do you know what? We're going to England. Come quick, Mother will tell you!" I rush home to hear more about this exciting news, and find Mother lying on the sofa, with a headache!

No wonder! The news has come like a bombshell, and the thought of packing and moving in winter with a family of seven children between the ages of six and seventeen temporarily stuns mother's strong constitution.

Father is now a renowned Salvationist composer, and the appointment back to England is to head up the Army's international music editorial department. Though my parents are Britishers, and recognize the significance of the appointment, there is a reluctance to leave Canada at this point in their lives. Canada is a great country in which to raise children even in the Depression years. Not only will life be more stringent in England, but there are already the darkening skies of threatening war.

For me, my brothers and sister, however, it is all excitement and adventure as we contemplated a new future. A seven-day voyage, for instance, has fascinating prospects. Brother Ray, in wonderment, makes the youthful observation, "Won't we have to make a lot of sandwiches!"

It is from Toronto Temple that we receive a musical send-off, with items contributed by Earslcourt, Dovercourt and Temple musical sections. Father has been particularly associated with these corps during our Toronto years. A report in *The War Cry*, the Army's flagship paper, gives me my first printed publicity. It says, "Junior Dudley Coles, who read a Psalm, caused a ripple of merriment when he recited the line, 'This poor man cried, and the Lord heard him.'" I can't imagine what kind of inflection I gave to that line.

We are given a grand send off from Union Station, and find a band waiting to give us a musical 'au revoire' at Hamilton as we pass through en route to New York. The winter journey across the Atlantic has faded from memory, but the cheerless atmosphere of our arrival in England is still remembered. Britain is plunged into mourning with the death of King George V, and London, shrouded in rain and darkened skies, dismally adds to the melancholy atmosphere. Further, it is disheartening to discover that no accommodation is immediately available. Temporary arrangements have been made for our accommodation at a Salvation Army hostel on Liverpool Street. Father is not exactly overjoyed to march his large family into a dining room crowded with down-and-outs for a first meal in England of fish and chips!

Perhaps it is the size of our family that presents a problem to the Army's administration, but Father acts quickly. He finds temporary accommodation at Edgware, and then takes out a mortgage to begin buying a house in Harrow, Middlesex. How he manages this I'll never know. But I do know that while our parents are fully committed to the Army and its service, they are equally dedicated to making a loving and happy home life for their children.

That first summer in England, for instance, Father is so keen that we should all have a short seaside holiday that he cashes an insurance policy to take us to Broadstairs, Kent, on the southeast coast. Of necessity, apparently, we travel on a Sunday (not the usual thing for Salvationists to do in those days) and I vividly remember the paddle steamer that takes us down the River Thames from Tilbury to Margate. That evening we are given our first glimpse of the sea, and take off our shoes and stockings to walk on the sandy beach and water's edge, before trekking a mile back to our holiday billet.

Problems arise, and adjustments are faced as we settle into England. For me, I sit for grammar school exams almost immediately—and fail. But how can I know how much it would cost to buy three-and-three-quarter yards of material at seven shillings and threepence-three-farthings a yard? I have no idea. I am struggling enough with dollars and cents. A little later, Father has Alan and me sit for a scholarship to the Trinity College of Music. Part of the exam includes rendering a self-chosen musical item. Alan, a little older than me, had learned to play the horn, and does well—he passes. Then two young women examiners listen with patient forbearance as I seek to bring winsome persuasiveness to my vocal rendition of "Drink to me only with thine eyes..." Unbelievably, they are not impressed. I fail, and disappoint my father again.

I always make a point of emphasizing that I was educated at Harrow, like Lord Byron and Sir Winston Churchill. I conveniently forget to mention that our schools are different, significantly. However, in the summer of 1939 I win a scholarship to a polytechnic commercial school in London, and brighter scholastic days seem to be ahead. Then war becomes imminent and officials decide to evacuate the school to Northampton, about 70 miles north of London.

Mother and Father have a difficult decision to make about their 13-year-old son. Reluctantly, they pack a little bag for me, and see me off on a train that will take me, with all my schoolmates away from the expected dangers of remaining in

London. Two days later, September 3, 1939, Prime Minister Neville Chamberlain declares war on Germany.

### A Boy in Wartime England

On arrival in Northampton we are paraded in pairs up and down several streets allocated to our school. Our teachers knock on the doors of little dwellings jammed together, and abutting the sidewalk. We come to a dwelling with a glass door and a sign that says, 'Off-licence.' A man with a glass eye appears with a plumpish wife. "We'll take two," they say. By this time I am at the head of the line with a bigger boy. This is a horrifying moment for me, because I have never been near a tavern of any kind in my life before. Salvationists abhor liquor, and the glass eye scares me, too. My fears quickly dispel, however, as we are welcomed into the hearts and home of two generous and good people.

After the first weekend, higher authorities rearrange all the evacuees, and with my schoolmate I am reassigned to the attractive home of successful business people who own two pork shops. I cannot fault the kindness which prompts them to receive us, but the home lacks the warmth of our earlier host and hostess.

There is also a brief stay at the home of an old, widowed Salvationist. Then the school decided to re-open in London after the Christmas break for those who wish to return. No severe air attack on Britain's capital city has yet occurred. I am happy to return home, even though heavy bombing of London did commence within a few months.

The next two years hold plenty of excitement for a young person like myself. I travel from Harrow by London-bound train to Kilburn, and then walk a mile to school. Often we leave the train due to bomb damage on the track and take a special bus to the next station. Most of many days is spent in the school's basement, and often gas masks are worn for practise purposes.

Father decides to erect our Anderson shelter in the living room, so Mother and Joan, with Norm, Ray and I, spend our nights there. In this 10' x 6' corrugated iron shelter, we're about as comfortable as tinned sardines. It is better, though, than marching out into the garden as many others do every time the air raid warning sounds.

In spite of all the difficulties, I learn much that has stood me in good stead all through the years, including shorthand, typing, commerce, bookkeeping and other general subjects. I begin my third year as a prefect, but choose to discontinue schooling during the year in order to accept a job offered me at Canada House, Trafalgar Square. It is the office of the High Commissioner for Canada, the Rt. Hon. Vincent Massey, P.C. My life opens to a new world, more exciting than anything known before.

As a secretarial assistant, I often type out long dispatches to the secretary of state for external affairs in Ottawa. It is a laborious task as five copies require four sheets of carbon paper, and the correction of mistakes is a frustrating exercise. Soon, however, I am called into the office of the official secretary, Frederick Hudd, and advised that I am being moved into the code and cypher office. The confidential nature of the work is impressed upon me and I am required to swear on a Bible that I will not divulge secret information. I sign a statement affirming this.

The closest I come to a slip up is the night I tell my parents to listen to the radio the next morning. When they do they hear the announcement of the Dieppe raid in which Canadian soldiers played a large part. Exciting days follow as I learn to handle the various codes, from simplest to most complex. It is a tedious task to add or subtract five-digit sequences of figures and then translate these into the words of an urgent top-secret cable for the High Commissioner. But greatly satisfying. Soon we progress to large electric machines that have a typewriter-style keyboard. Inside are five cylindrical drums, each with multiple settings that are changed daily. These

Typex machines enable us better to cope with the voluminous cable traffic, but we worked many late nights nonetheless.

George Ignatieff and Charles R. Ritchie are two members of the High Commissioner's staff who become well-known diplomats in ensuing years. A number of times I take secret messages to the Commonwealth Offices situated through an arch opposite Winston Churchill's residence at 10 Downing Street. I have a special pass for this.

Meantime, it is 'business as usual' at home, too, in spite of frequent bombings, all-night raids, rationing, queuing, and all the other dangers and difficulties of a lengthy war. We younger folk find it more exciting than fearful to cycle to the Salvation Army corps on Sundays with shrapnel from British guns falling around us. Occasionally we will actually see a low-flying German plane just before it is shot down. We live just a few miles from Northolt Airport, a fighter airfield. Even our nightly turns of 'air raid watching' have their element of excitement, as we walk our street at all hours with fire bucket, flashlight and log book, and watch for incendiary bombs.

But we little comprehend the anxiety faced by parents. Mother and Father surely are examples of British courage and heroism. Gordon, my eldest brother, is called up for military service immediately war is declared, and has arrived in Singapore by Christmas 1939. He is reported missing after the fall of Singapore in February 1942, and it is not until 18 months later that a card arrives from him in Japan with a marvelous six-word message: "Keeping well, always cheerful, love Gordon." He is 23 and had survived appalling experiences. He will remain a prisoner of war for two more years, working in a coal mine for 14 hours a day.

Meantime, Bramwell (the next eldest) has joined the Royal Air Force and qualified as a navigator. Joan, my sister, joins the Women's Royal Naval Service (WRENS), and is posted to New

York where she becomes a petty officer. Alan is called up a little later and joins a tank regiment. He later drives heavy transportation vehicles through several European countries, following the invasion. I am next, and before my eighteenth birthday have joined the Royal Navy. On my first night at sea I experience action off the coast of Southern France.

The stoic courage of people like Mother and Father needs to be highlighted. They have no idea what their children are doing, what crises they are facing, how they are coping. My address is "c/o G.P.O. London" and all letters are severely censored. We cannot say where we are or what is happening. The anxiety of parents is hard to imagine.

Through 1943, I write to my sister in New York a long newsy letter each month. As I read some of them again I realize how much the Salvation Army corps at Harrow, and in particular the corps cadet brigade (a young people's Bible study and evangelism group) help to shape my life in those formative years. We are a happy, fun-loving, mixed group of young folk who are challenged to grow spiritually in faith and service, in the congenial and supportive atmosphere of peer friendship. And we seem to enjoy each other's company without getting into serious relationships of any kind. Society is not so sexually-absorbed as it is today.

I wonder now at the energy and enthusiasm we put into religious activities. True, we do not have TV and the multiplicity of recreational distractions offered today, but I cannot believe we are less happy. I work six days a week (often with late nights), face difficulty or even danger getting home because of air raids—and then without reluctance or hesitation devote a full Sunday to Salvation Army activities. This includes a band outdoor meeting on a nearby street to start the day, followed by a march back to the hall and the regular morning service. Then the bandsmen (I play trombone) rush to an afternoon outdoor meeting in a more distant district, before cycling home for a quick tea. Finally there is one more outdoor meeting and march of witness, indoor service, and short praise-style 'wind-up' meeting to end the day.

Of course, because of bombing raids primarily during hours of darkness, it is necessary to cancel evening activities during the winter months. Often the air raids would start as we cycle home in the late afternoon. A danger which we hardly consider is the shrapnel which falls around us from our own military defence guns. We compete with each other to collect the biggest pieces.

### Wartime Service in the Royal Navy

Not surprisingly, I take my faith seriously as evident in my letter to Joan just a month before joining the Royal Navy, and three months before my 18$^{th}$ birthday: "How do I feel? Well, I don't know—except to say that once they get me in uniform the war will soon be over! Seriously though, there is one thing I am determined about, and that is that my service years will not be wasted. I am determined to use this time profitably, in general and spiritual terms, so that on being discharged after hostilities cease, I can look back upon these years and say that I am a better man for having seen service in the Royal Navy. I pray that God will help me."

Even amid the horror of war, that prayer is wonderfully answered. After general training on England's east coast near Harwich (*H.M.S. Ganges*), and specialized radar training on the western Isle of Man, I return to my central barracks at Chatham in southern England for posting. The very day I report to Chatham after a few days' leave, I am given a train ticket to Plymouth, on the southwest coast. Arriving at the renowned seaport and naval base, a motorboat quickly takes me to join the ship's crew of a British cruiser, *H.M.S. Mauritius*. She is anchored out in the Sound, under the watchful eye of Sir Francis Drake's monument, high on the Hoe.

Within a couple of hours we take up our anchor and slowly move out to sea, heading for the French coast. The beach landings took place a few weeks earlier, and *Mauritius* has given tactical support to land troops in the embattled inland area of Caen. Our cruiser can fire her 12 six-inch guns more than 20,000 yards with ease. As, on successive days, the battles move further inland, we operate further south. An official record of those days tells me, for instance, that on the night of $15^{th}$-$16^{th}$ August 1944—my first on board—we are patrolling with the Canadian destroyers *Ursa* and *Iroquois* in the vicinity of the enemy-occupied base at La Rochelle. As anticipated, contact is made with enemy shipping, and in the ensuing engagement two minesweepers and three merchant ships are sunk, and one escorting destroyer hit. Exactly a week later, further south in Audierne Bay between Brest and Lorient, we destroy eight enemy ships. Other actions take place around the mouth of the Gironde River, as well as just south of St. Nazaire.

It isn't long, however, before we are steaming up the length of the British Isles to join the Home Fleet at its renowned base at Scapa Flow, in the Orkney Isles. Scapa is cold, barren and isolated from civilization. Yet, to a ship's company returning from an arduous mission in Arctic and North Atlantic waters, it is a welcome haven of rest and peace amid dangerous waters. Etched in memory is a miserable winter run to Iceland, with urgent secret equipment lashed to the decks. We face gale conditions so severe that two days later we cannot enter the harbour at Reykjavik, and have to anchor in a fiord in the north of the island. Throughout the week or so at sea, the cooks can only give us soup and tea. What heavenly bliss it is when our ice-caked ship passes through the boom defence at Scapa Flow once again.

We take part in a number of engagements up the Norwegian coast from the Skaggerak to Spitzbergen during those early winter months, sometimes alone, sometimes in a task force that includes an aircraft carrier and six destroyers. Some of these destroyers are Canadian, one being the famed, *H.M.C.S. Sioux*. But it is at the end of January 1945 that *Mauritius* finishes her impressive record of wartime action. The action is worth describing in some detail.

The ship's company is enjoying a well-deserved rest that Saturday afternoon when over the loudspeaker we hear the unexpected call to prepare to leave harbour. Within the hour we have climbed out of hammocks, stowed away partly-washed clothing, cleared the decks and moved to our sea stations. With another cruiser, *H.M.S. Diadem*, behind us we slide quietly out of Scapa Flow and head north-east toward the Norwegian coast.

After an action station rehearsal, a voice comes over the ship's loudspeaker system once again: "This is the captain speaking. You will be glad to know that we are shortly to engage the enemy. Three German destroyers have been sighted steaming south near Trondheimsfiord and we expect to engage them about midnight." Some further words of advice in the Nelson tradition ("Every man is expected to do his duty!") follow, and then we return to our normal wartime sea watches.

Those of us who are off watch in my mess deck engage in heated discussion about what the night might hold for us. Suppressed fear and excitement are dominant emotions felt by most of my companions as evening hours approach. I am not quite 19, and the average age of the ship's company is likely less than 25.

I had faced some mocking and resistance when first opening my Bible and praying on the mess deck six months earlier. But not now. Many of my colleagues are supportive and, in fact, woe betide anyone who interferes with the devotional moments I feel to be so important and necessary. And on this night I am surprised and encouraged by a request to read and pray with my able-seaman comrades—all of us so soon to face danger and the possibility of death. Few are atheists when they go into battle, and there is a genuine reaching up to God for courage and protection through the dangerous hours ahead.

All too soon we are called to action stations. It is midnight and a half-moon plays hide and seek between the slow-moving clouds. I am down in the bowels of the ship in what is called the transmission station. It is primarily manned by eight members of the ship's small Royal Marine contingent. The marines stand around a large 'table' into which myriad pieces of information are constantly fed: range, bearing, inclination, rate of change of range, effect of wind on shell, deflections and variations of all sorts. Through complicated computations (in a pre-computer age) the gun turrets are automatically fed the information needed to fire accurately at a designated target. My job is to feed into the 'table' an accurate present range and bearing passed down to my monitor from an upper deck radar office.

To be frank, we little know what is happening through the next two hours of battle, though the room itself is a hive of intense and purposeful activity. The suppressed tension we all feel is modified by the calm and authoritative leadership of the warrant officer in charge. Not till later do I know that 18 torpedoes have been fired at our two British ships—and all missed! Nor do I realize that my own messdeck has been hit by gunfire and my friends and I have lost all our clothes and personal belongings.

Eventually the loudspeaker crackles again: "This is the captain speaking. You will be sorry to know the engagement has been broken off with the enemy ships escaping up a fiord. All have been hit. We and our sister ship have also suffered some damage. There have been some injuries, one rating has died. That will be all." In actual fact none of us is sorry the battle has ended. Rather, we cheer when the captain adds that we are heading full speed for home.

There is a moving moment when at 11 o'clock on that crisp Sunday morning we all assemble on the quarterdeck, our sister ship alongside, engines to slow, while the body of the dead sailor, wrapped in a Union Jack flag, slides silently into the water. Prayers are said, a bugler sounds The Last Post, and the two ships—still in danger from air and undersea attack—move back to full speed, heading for the comparative safety of Scapa Flow.

Soon after return to Scapa, the *Mauritius* is sent down to Gladstone dock in Liverpool for repairs. The damage to my messdeck is not a big problem, but in that final action we force our boilers beyond capacity and some major engine room repairs are necessary. The ship is decommissioned, and I am one of the few remaining on board as C. & M. (care and maintenance) party. I become office secretary to the executive officer who takes charge of the ship.

When the war ends all ships of the home fleet are invited to European ports to share in victory celebrations. I am disappointed to spend V.E. (Victory in Europe) night patrolling the dry dock where a forlorn-looking *Mauritius* now rests. My duty is to prevent inebriated sailors who have been over-zealous in their celebrations, from falling in. Hardly the most exciting night of my life!

A reader of these recollections may wonder how, as a Christian, I can seemingly take pride in my war experiences. Doesn't Scripture support non-violence? Certainly I ponder the ethics of war more deeply than I did as an 18-year-old. I believe that Christians are called to resist evil, but agree a central issue arises over the means to be adopted.

Through the centuries, a Christian 'just war' theory has been developed, and Augustine, Thomas Aquinas and Hugo Grotius are noteworthy among those who set out principles governing the use of arms to resist evil. These included sufficient cause, good intention, discrimination and proportion. While the former two would seem to be unarguable in the Second World War, the basic principles of discrimination and proportion were soon abandoned. In Britain we faced five long years of havoc-wreaking warfare before Victory in Europe Day was celebrated with indescribable joy.

But another fierce, unconquered enemy in the Far East still had to be faced, and enormous Allied casualties were expected. Our huge relief that the war ended so abruptly was tempered, of course, by the loss of lives in Hiroshima and Nagasaki. Some argue that no less lives might have been lost had the atomic bomb not made history.

Within a few decades nuclear weapons, far exceeding the power of that first atomic bomb, have now brought humanity to an historical crossroads. Nuclear weapons (including chemical and biological weapons) being indiscriminate in their effects are immoral, and indefensible in their use. A nuclear war could never be a just war. And there would be no winners.

What is clear to me is that Christians must not abdicate their responsibility to participate in the ongoing task of aiding the peaceful resolution of global problems. We must be strong in upholding the biblical truth that righteousness exalts a nation. "Blessed are the peacemakers" is still good advice to share with a world lurching from one crisis to another, and to live out individually in the relational tensions of everyday life.

### *Much to Ponder*

For a 19-year-old, now standing on the threshold of a new life in which he tries to shape his own destiny, there is much to ponder. Many opportunities and possibilities to be considered. Many choices to think about. Choices decide destinies. What part will I allow my roots, my home and family influences, my wartime experiences to play in shaping future decisions? What course must I set for the immediate future?

No wonder I am restless as I ponder an unknown future. It will take several years for a resolution of these questions. I will become increasingly aware that good choices must have significant purpose and be based on worthy principles.

Yes, it will take several restless years before the pivotal point is discovered. And once discovered, it will open life to many other moments when significant choices and decisions have to be made that reinforce, or diminish the effectiveness of, the pivotal point.

My experience of warfare, coupled to subsequent reflection and divine prodding, leads me a little later to a lifelong, better fight in an Army without guns, The Salvation Army. And that leap of faith has already been recounted!

## *REFLECTIONS*

What unusual experiences are mine as I journey through these tumultuous years! Normal home life is quickly disrupted. Bombings, emergency situations and curtailed activities are a backdrop to growing toward adulthood in wartime England.

Completing schooling in bomb shelters, the beginning of employment, and service in His Majesty's Royal Navy must leave some mark on one's life. Harsh training days in the Navy are certainly a wake-up call to the raw edge of life. Our training instructors are intentionally hardened men whose job is to prepare us for the ugliness of war. They curse and swear at any clumsiness demonstrated or any slowness in obeying commands.

Wartime actions in the English Channel, Bay of Biscay, North Sea, Norwegian Sea and North Atlantic all contribute to making me the kind of person I became on discharge, and as I begin to shape my own future. Where would it lead? Initially, to restlessness.

## Conclusion

As I have reflected on choices and decisions in a Christian life, what new insights have I gained? What conclusions reached? I ponder a few.

While hereditary and heritage have unarguable significance, they do not necessarily decide the life journey to follow. There are countless examples of individuals not measuring up to their privileged heritage, and conversely individuals deprived of heritage and opportunity nevertheless rising to remarkable heights of achievement and influence. Personally, I recognize, and thank God for, the enviable influences that surrounded me in formative years.

A Christian lifestyle that involves a personal encounter with Christ can be a bedrock of certainty. Memorized Scripture can be a bulwark against doubts and indecision. Three that have meant much to Eva and me through the years still hang on our walls:

> *Ezekiel 11:16 (KJV): "Yet shall I be to them as a little sanctuary in the countries where they shall come." (We sometimes insert 'situations' for 'countries'!)*

> *Romans 8:28: "And we know that all things work together for good to those who love God..." (My NIV Bible gives as an alternative translation, "God works together with those who love Him to bring about what is good.")*

> *Galatians 5:22,2 (RV): "The fruit of the Spirit is love, joy, peace, patience, kindness, goodness, faithfulness, meekness, self-control:"*

Prayer will establish the attitude with which each day is faced. As well as ad hoc prayers, formal published prayers of others can stretch and challenge our own hearts and minds. For many years, Leslie D. Weatherhead's *A Private House of Prayer* was a faithful companion to my prayer life.

For me, faith to be strong and realistic requires a spiritually adventurous disposition. Ships alongside the harbour wall may look impressive, but that's not what ships are for. It is outside harbour walls, facing the ever-changing seas that their true mission is accomplished. 'We must make choices that enable us to fulfill the deepest capacities of our real selves,' said Thomas Merton.

Never be afraid of making mistakes. We can learn from them. There is no such thing as Christian infallibility. To quote Canon John Young again: "In one sense God has a fresh 'plan' for our lives every morning, no matter how great the mess and muddle we've made of life thus far. God never gives up on us. He does not offer us a blueprint. Instead God offers us himself."

'It takes plenty of courage to live according to one's convictions,' says Paul Tournier. 'That is why it is always so difficult to break away from social conformity, to act differently from everybody else.' I am somewhat amazed as I reflect on my decision to kneel and pray on the messdeck of my ship as a young seaman. Would I do it again today?

Underlying every decisive choice there is necessarily a prior, fundamental choice, a spiritual one, says Tournier. 'It is the choice of one's God—whether that be yourself, your instincts, your pleasure, reason, science—or Jesus Christ.' It is the spiritual factor that gives man his value.

Swiss psychiatrist Paul Tournier adds to this thought the comment that the Christian scale of values does not deny the importance of psychological factors. It contains them, and goes beyond them. To experience the 'new birth' of which the Lord speaks (John 3:3) is indeed to become adult, to attain to the fullness of humanity ordained by God.

If, then, this autobiography has fulfilled its purpose, it will have enhanced awareness of a loving God's gracious hand remarkably guiding two solitary souls through the twentieth century and beyond. We pray it will also encourage and persuade others to launch out on a similar, immeasurably rewarding, faith journey. Essentially, life at its best is a matter of good choices. And the best choices start, as they did for Eva and me, by echoing George Matheson's inspired and transforming words:

> *O Love that wilt not let me go,*
> *I rest my weary soul in thee;*
> *I give thee back the life I owe*
> *That in thine ocean depths its flow*
> *May richer, fuller be.*

---

*To order additional copies or to contact the author,*
*please visit:*
www.colespublishing.com

Royal Navy Ordinary Seaman Dudley Coles, Age 17.

Dudley's ship, the cruiser *HMS Mauritius*.

After six years of separation, Coles family reunites to welcome Gordon from P.O.W. camp in Japan.

Raymond, Dudley, Gordon, Alan, Bram, Joan, Father, Mother and Norman.

# EARLY YEARS 1943-1955

Royal Canadian Mounted Police head Canadian contingent in 1953 Coronation procession. Canada House on extreme right.

Rt. Hon. Vincent Massey with staff at Canada House. Dudley sitting in centre.

Berlin Airlift, Aircraft re-load and refuel, 1948/49.

Dudley's Grandpa, Brigadier Edwin LeButt (*left*) when private secretary to Chief of Staff, Bramwell Booth (*right*).

Dudley and Eva both commissioned as Probationary Lieutenants, June 28 1954.

Post wedding photo (*l-r*): Eva's brother Ernie, Mum Beth, Eva, Dudley & Dad Rollie Oxbury.

*OFF TO INDIA 1959-1973* 171

Farewells at Union Station with Father (*left*) and Faith & brother Norman, on our departure for India, June 1959.

At Montreal Pier dockside, Eva, Dudley and baby Heather are seen off by Major George Heron.

On board *RMS Saxonia* heading up the St. Lawrence River, June 1959.

Dudley, Eva & baby Heather in front yard in Poona soon after arrival in India, 1959.

Dudley playing with the children: Heather & baby Howard in Poona, 1961.

Salesmen and entertainers of all sorts show up at our front yard in Poona. Here a snake charmer with flute and his cobra.

The small metre guage, steam-engine hill train travels up the Blue Mountains to the S.A. Surrenden 'home of rest' in the Nilgiri Hills, 1962.

Graham, almost 5, joins Howard and Heather at boarding school, 1967.

Graham smiles from a window of the train taking many children to hill schools at Coonoor and Ootacamund, South India.

*174*  *OFF TO INDIA 1959-1973*

Eva chats to an Indian village family surrounded by onlookers.

An Indian village woman prepares meal.

Visiting a typical Indian village home; family and cattle live in close quarters.

Typical Bangladesh rush hour.

*OFF TO INDIA 1959-1973* 175

Married cadets of the Lightbringers training session in Anand, Gujerat, 1972.

S.A Projects include: Feeding Programs, Digging Wells and Skills Training Programs

*176*                          *OFF TO INDIA 1959-1973*

S.A missionary families vacationing at Naini Tal, our first holiday in India.

◁ Our children, Heather, Howard and Graham with 4 school friends in the tea plantations on holiday.

▷
Heather, Howard and Graham in Anand, Gujerat 1971.

S.A. Canadian families enjoy annual May holidays together at "Surrenden", Coonoor, South India

# Back to Canada 177

Our family and friends on camels in Karachi.

On homeland furlough in Canada, we demonstrate Indian musical drums, clappers and harmonium.

Staff at S.A. Editorial office in Oakville, 1981.

Conference of South Asia leaders meets in South India. It is chaired by Commissioners Ron (Chief of Staff) & Hilda Cox (*front row, grey uniforms*).

General & Mrs. Jarl Walstrom take salute at Sri Lanka welcome parade.

In Toronto, Dudley & Eva are welcomed to Christian Children's Fund headquarters, and thank Peter Harris and staff for Sri Lanka sponsorship assistance.

Dudley, with Captain Bo Brekke, pauses at bed of young man injured in a Colombo, Sri Lanka, bomb blast.

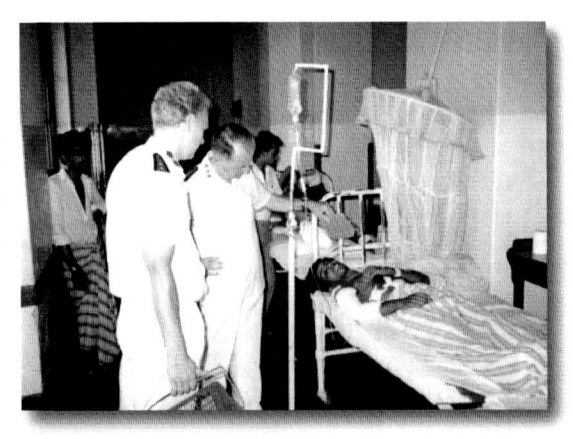

Friendship aircraft brings Dudley and Eva from Calcutta to a strong Salvationist presence in northeast India's isolated Mizoram.

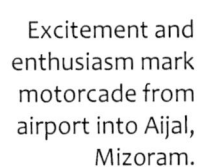

Excitement and enthusiasm mark motorcade from airport into Aijal, Mizoram.

Dudley and Eva visiting Afghan refugee programs at Peshawar, Pakistan.

Salvationists greet Dudley and Eva at S.A Girls Home, South West India.

Happy moments in South Eastern India.

Dudley at S.A. Community Health Centre in Jessore, Bangladesh.

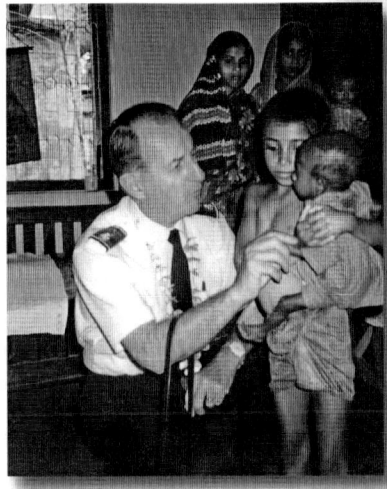

Dudley pauses to have a one way conversation with a young child at a family care centre.

Celebratory service at Rangoon Central Corps as the Burma division status is raised to 'independent command'.

Smiles and garlands during Dudley and Eva's retirement event conducted by General Eva Burrows at I.H.Q. London.

◁ In retirement, Dudley crews Bronte Yatch Club race committee boat, and hoists "change of course" flag.

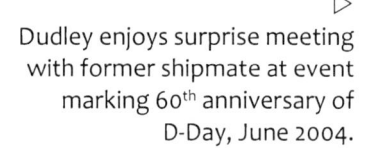

▷
Dudley enjoys surprise meeting with former shipmate at event marking 60th anniversary of D-Day, June 2004.

Dudley and Eva celebrate 50th wedding anniversary with three children, their three spouses, and eight grandchildren.